Praise for *Sheepish*

"*Sheepish* is as smart and funny as its title. Catherine Friend takes us along on her quest to master the other 'oldest profession.' Warning: It may make you want to drop everything and go tend a flock."
—Meg Daly Olmert, author of *Made for Each Other: The Biology of the Human-Animal Bond*

"Wry, witty, and honest, *Sheepish* describes a magical personal transformation—from urban to rural. Catherine Friend finds meaning in the middle of life, love, and even knitting projects. Friend brings out the urge to farm in knitters, spinners, and 'fiber freaks' everywhere, teaching us to find joy and contentment in the small, sheepy parts of our world."
—Joanne Seiff, author of *Fiber Gathering* and *Knit Green*

Praise for *Hit by a Farm*

"A charming memoir . . . [with] magical moments."
—*New York Times Book Review*

"A thoroughly engaging romp for all. This is a must-read for any city girl who's ever whiled away an hour or two dreaming about the bucolic existence of her rural sisters."—*Bust*

"Heartening, sweet, earthy, funny—a joy to read from start to finish."
—*Minneapolis Star-Tribune*

"A funny farming guide: a book about two women who decide to go back to the land—and discover the realities of the land's hardships for non-rural residents. Whether it's dealing with broken fences and boundaries, stubborn sheep, or sheep who are gazelles in sheep's clothing, *Hit by a Farm* is filled with fun moments, accounts of overwork and mishaps, and more."—*Midwest Book Review*

"A multi-mood, clever and unpredictable tale of what makes farm life far from mundane and sheltered . . . *Hit by a Farm* slyly educates as it entertains, heals as it humors us while wading through issues of confrontation, complications, and compromise . . . a treasure."—*Madison Capital Times*

Praise for *The Compassionate Carnivore*

"Smart, personal, and funny, *The Compassionate Carnivore* will make you want to hug a cow—and order a ribeye."—*Women's Health*

"[Friend's] words give hope to those of us who crave meat, but are sickened by some modern farming practices."—*Curve*

"*The Compassionate Carnivore* is both an entertaining memoir and a chapter-by-chapter breakdown of how America raises its meat. . . . Yes, much of this is as grim as it is familiar—but Friend manages to make it lively and even funny without burying her essential moral seriousness."
—*Culinate*

"I loved Catherine Friend's philosophy on how to be a compassionate carnivore, and I cried when I read the chapter 'Letter to My Lambs.' It really is possible to deeply care about animals and eat meat."
—Temple Grandin, author of *Animals in Translation*

"Full of interesting facts . . . "—*Guardian*

"Friend's direct, yet tactful approach will educate without making the reader feel judged for their decision to be a carnivore. It's an informative and at times funny approach to get people to think about what they eat and the process meat goes through before it gets to your freezer. Our choices have an effect not just on the animals, but on our health and environment. If you have been struggling with eating meat for health reasons or personal convictions, *The Compassionate Carnivore* will help you."
—*Blogcritics*

"Filled with insightful and often humorous anecdotes. When not horrifying me with various practices of making meat ready for market . . . Friend had me roaring with laughter. . . . Backed by research, practical experience, and the desire to improve standards, Friend offers many sound suggestions. If more carnivores demand humanely raised meat, the supply will hopefully follow."—*Story Circle Book Reviews*

"In this deeply personal account of her involvement in the humane raising of sheep, self-described shepherd, animal lover, and committed carnivore Catherine Friend leads us through the lives of meat animals—in our industrial food system, and on her farm—with metaphor, compassion, and wit. A rich and enjoyable read."
—Joan Dye Gussow, author of *This Organic Life*

sheepish

Also by Catherine Friend

sheepish

Two Women, Fifty Sheep, and
Enough Wool to Save the Planet

CATHERINE FRIEND

Da Capo

LIFE
LONG
A Member of the Perseus Books Group

Design and production by Trish Wilkinson
Set in 11 point Goudy Old Style

Library of Congress Cataloging-in-Publication Data

Friend, Catherine.
  Sheepish : two women, fifty sheep, and enough wool to save the planet / Catherine Friend. — 1st Da Capo Press ed.
    p.   cm.
  ISBN 978-0-306-81844-8
  1. Friend, Catherine. 2. Sheep ranchers—Minnesota—Biography. 3. Women shepherds—Minnesota—Biography. 4. Women farmers—Minnesota—Biography. 5. Wool industry—Minnesota. 6. Sheep ranches—Minnesota. 7. Farm life—Minnesota. 8. Minnesota—Social life and customs. 9. Minnesota—Biography. I. Title.
  SF375.32.F73A3 2011
  630.9776—dc22   2010048194

First Da Capo Press edition 2011

Published by Da Capo Press
A Member of the Perseus Books Group
www.dacapopress.com

10 9 8 7 6 5 4 3 2 1

For our pasture goddesses
Amelia Hansa, Mary Hoff, and Bonnie Mueller

Contents

PART 1
The Muffins Go Farming

PART 2
Telling Farm Tales

PART 3
Spinning Yarns

PART 4
Unravel

PART 5
The Love of You Sings

We are all sheep mad in this part of the country, and I am really become very sheepish myself.

—WILLIAM THORNTON,
IN A LETTER TO HIS FELLOW SHEPHERD
THOMAS JEFFERSON, MAY 10, 1810

PART

ONE

The Muffins Go Farming

Shocking

Hang warning signs on the electric fence at
critical areas where children or *untrained* adults
will encounter the fence.

—PREMIER ONE FENCE SUPPLIES

The man and woman are young, perhaps in their late twenties,
and I'm giving them a brief tour of our farm before we transact
business—they're here to buy beef. As we stand near the fence
watching the sheep, the man looks down at the smooth wire running from post to post.

"Is this electric?"

I nod. There's a yellow sign hanging from the top wire about
thirty feet away. The sign says, "Warning: Electric Fence."

"What happens if I touch it?"

I look straight at him and tighten my jaw so I won't laugh. The
nearest sheep chews her cud and eavesdrops. She is No. 66, the

eldest of the flock, which means she's been around the pasture a few times. I know what she's thinking as she watches the man fixate on the fence: *And people think* we're *stupid?*

I turn back to the young man. "The fence charger pulses one second on, one second off, so you have a fifty-fifty chance of nothing happening. Or 5,000 volts could race up your arm, surge through your chest and down your legs into the ground."

He can't take his eyes off the fence. "Would it hurt?"

The guy's wife rolls her eyes. "Honey, don't touch the fence."

I explain that yes, it will hurt. It won't kill him, but he might cry out for his mommy for the first time in years. I try to move the couple back toward the driveway, but the man remains transfixed. I sigh.

After fifteen years on this farm, I've been zapped repeatedly by this fence, sometimes in very private places. Every animal on this farm respects the fence. When lambs are young they cluster close to the fence, investigating. One will eventually touch a wire with its wool-free nose, shoot straight up in the air, bleat louder than it's ever bleated before, then race for Mama. The rest of the lambs scatter in panic, and just like that, they've been trained. That slender wire is now Scary Place, to be avoided at all costs.

Our border collie, Robin, understands the fence. In his prime, that guy could jump fences. After we'd finish herding the sheep into new pasture, he'd stand at the thirty-two-inch wire fence, watching me in anticipation, then I'd give the command "Over," and he'd leap like a gazelle, clearing those electric fences by at least a foot. It was an impressive sight.

Robin did this partly because he was so athletic and graceful, but also because over the years he'd developed a healthy respect for the electric fence and knew that if he didn't clear the fence, a scary jolt of something painful would follow.

One winter day after Robin and I had done chores, I asked him to cross the fence he'd jumped dozens of times before. Unfortunately, the ice or snow affected his launch, so as he leaped, it became clear he wasn't going to make it all the way over. I knew it. He knew it.

That was why he started screaming in midair, knowing his tender belly (or his even more tender private boy parts) were about to land on a pulsing 5,000-volt fence. His front feet landed on the ground, and sure enough, his hips hung up on the top wire. The poor guy was draped over the fence, really screaming now.

I stood there, waiting, since I knew something he didn't. The electricity was off.

In a few seconds he figured it out and stopped screaming. He gave a few kicks to get off the wire, then walked over to a pile of snow and peed in a manly way.

We haven't spoken of the incident since.

My partner, Melissa, has regular but always surprising contact with the fence. One spring day, I'm on one side of a nonelectric red metal gate and she's on the other. We're talking about how strong the fence current is this year, almost 8,000 volts instead of the usual 5,000. I'm about to reach through the gate and hug her when she suddenly screams, flings herself back, rolls twice, then curls up in a ball in the grass. There is a fencing switch near the gate, and Melissa has accidentally touched a hot bolt with her wrist. I'm so sorry she's been shocked. I'm also a bit relieved we weren't touching when it happened, since one should take the concept of sharing only so far. I murmur sympathetically through the gate, afraid to touch it in case it's hot. After a few moans she climbs to her feet, shakes herself, and takes some deep breaths.

"You okay?" I ask.

"I feel rebooted," she says. She's amazing. Shoot 8,000 volts through her entire body, and she's on her feet in minutes, rebooted and refreshed.

I don't share these stories with the young man and his wife because he doesn't want to hear them. The man leans over to examine the top wire. Electricity is invisible, which makes it *really* hard to believe in.

"Will it hurt *much?*" Because people are fascinated by farms, we want visitors to feel comfortable establishing a connection with ours on any level. This guy wants not just an emotional contact, but a literal one as well.

I shrug. "I find it unpleasant."

He reaches out and touches the fence. Nothing happens. Because he isn't going to be satisfied until he's been shocked, he touches the fence again.

The guy leaps back, clutching his hand, too stunned to swear. His eyes expand from human eyes to wildly spinning cartoon eyes. If I hadn't been standing there, he might have folded himself into his wife's arms and whimpered.

"You okay?"

"Oh yeah, sure." The guy, now trained to the fence, straightens his manly shoulders and ambles away, in need of a private moment.

The word most people would use to describe the expression on his face is "sheepish."

Sheepishness

"The Things We Do for Love"
—SONG BY 10CC

Most of us use the word "sheepish" to mean embarrassed, ashamed, or chagrined. Sheep, however, are never embarrassed, ashamed, or chagrined. Not ever. So this definition makes absolutely no sense.

Instead of interpreting the "-ish" suffix to mean "like," as in "like a sheep," another possibility is "of or belonging to." Think: *Spanish*—of or belonging to Spain. *Danish*—of or belonging to fruit-filled pastries.

Sheepish—of or belonging to sheep.

Sixteen years ago I was not at *all* sheepish. I was bookish, library-ish, wine-and-appetizer-ish. Decidedly unsheepish. My only exposure to sheep was as a child visiting my grandmother's sheep ranch in southeastern Montana—lots of dust, lots of heat, and every now and then a little orphan lamb that I could help Grandma feed with a bottle. My grandmother left the ranch when I was a teenager, so sheep played no role in my life after that.

As an adult, I met Melissa through a personal ad, the pre-Internet method for dating. She and I were totally different, not two people who should build a life together, so we fell in love and did precisely that. We led fairly boring, urban lives for over ten years while I discovered writing and Melissa cultivated her love of land and animals and caring for both.

Then, out of the blue, Melissa asked me if I would help her start a farm.

I gave her question some thought. I knew nothing about animals, I didn't like hard labor, and I didn't like getting my hands dirty. "Sure," I said, "let's start a farm." Less than two years later, I was plopped down into the middle of a strange, undiscovered country filled with sheep, lambs, goats, llamas, chicken poop, and more blood than I was comfortable with. As new farmers, we amused our friends and family with creative disasters. We accidentally overdosed and nearly killed all our sheep one week. We forgot to check the oil in the tractor engine, with quite expensive results. Melissa nearly shish-kebabed herself when a sharp-toothed implement called a drag crawled up behind her on the tractor. I cleverly planted 200 grapevines upside down. We had to learn about sheep and duck penises. That I even *know* about pizzle rot disturbs me. We healed the sick animals we could and buried those we couldn't. We committed to raising sheep the old-fashioned way, letting them graze fresh grass every day, letting them give birth outside in the spring instead of inside a barn during the winter.

Everything was new. The first time Melissa left our animals in my care, she called me the next morning from her brother's house in Illinois, her voice as casual as she could make it. "So, how are the animals?"

"Oh yeah, about that," I replied, voice just as calm. "They're all dead."

Sharp inhale. Long pause. Weak laugh.

"Ha. Very funny. You had me going there."

I puffed up with pride because it's really difficult to stun Melissa. After that, whenever Melissa leaves the farm overnight, she calls the next day and inquires after the animals.

"All dead," I reply sadly.

"Okay," she says. "Good job." Farmers are far too comfortable with black humor.

Melissa and I eventually moved away from the chaos. The farm found its rhythm and beat steadily, a comfort to us both. We moved from neophytes to experienced farmers. We raised animals and tended a one-acre vineyard. We acquired dozens of satisfied lamb customers, and vegetarian neighbors who bought most of our eggs.

As one who raises sheep, I call myself a shepherd. I also call myself Mrs. Muffin. Our friend Mary H. has known Melissa since second grade. When they get together, forty years slide off to reveal two eight-year-olds. They have nicknames for each other and can spend two hours on the phone without either of them taking a breath. I once found them in the kitchen wearing aluminum foil caps to protect their brains from the shrill whistle of our teakettle. Clearly it was too late; the damage had already been done.

One day I need to call Mary, so I use Melissa's cell phone.

"Muffin!" Mary crows, thinking she has Melissa on the phone.

"No, it's—"

"Mrs. Muffin!"

Yes, well, I guess so. The name sticks.

Farming has been a wild ride for Mrs. Muffin. Goats have kicked buckets of warm milk all over me. I've been glared at by angry llamas. I've been playfully chased by 800-pound steers and then thoroughly licked by those same steers after they cornered me. I've even been attacked by a duck, which is humiliating to admit. I don't know which hurt more—the duck clamped onto my pudgy knee or the knowledge that a duck could even do such a thing. *Ducks*, people. What kind of a world is this?

But the sheep, ah, the sheep. After caring for them so many years, I fear I might have fallen under their spell. I like spending time with them. I like patting their heads and scratching behind their ears. I like nuzzling their babies against my neck. I like the challenge of convincing 150 animals to move in the same direction.

Unfortunately, I find it extremely hard to combine a writing life and a farming life. As author and farmer E. B. White wrote, "I have drifted farther and farther from my muse, closer and closer to my post-hole digger." I know how he felt. Once we started farming, my muse took one look at my dirt-stained hands and manure-encrusted boots, and she delicately and oh-so-politely explained she had an engagement elsewhere. I believe she flitted off to England. (J. K. Rowling, I'd like my muse back. Thanks.)

After overdosing our sheep and blowing up the tractor engine and planting the grapevines upside down, I sit down one evening at my computer and type *How Not to Farm*. Because we are making every mistake in the book, I might as well write that book. I compose a little piece about my idiotic vineyard experience and bring it to my writing group. They laugh, which is a tactical error because I then bring another little piece, and another. After a few more meetings, my friend Jane says I'm writing a memoir. I disagree, insisting that I'm only writing little pieces.

Museless, I keep writing. Two years and 300 pages later, I have written what turns out to be—why is Jane always right?—a memoir. I've even given it a catchy title: "Searching for Placenta by

Moonlight," based on Melissa's ability to walk through the pasture in the dark and find the placenta for a specific birth that took place that day. She knows exactly what she's doing out here. I don't.

Despite this, the act of writing about farming makes me aware of how rare, and how amazing, a life it is. As shepherds, Melissa and I lead the flock. We care for the sheep, we protect them. We are responsible for their health and well-being. They are our business, and so much more. People coyly refer to prostitution as the "oldest profession," but sheepherding goes back even further. When we sit in our pasture watching our sheep, Melissa and I are doing the same thing humans have done for 10,000 years. Stop and think of that. Ten *thousand* years.

Sheep have been around since before literature, so they've been written about from the beginning—Roman writings, nursery rhymes, bad poetry. Sheep are the stars of the Bible, showing up more than 500 times, and they're the first animal named in Genesis. David likened fleece to snow, and Solomon describes his mistress's teeth as "resembling a flock of sheep just come up from the washing." How many pick-up lines do you know that involve sheep? (Appropriate pick-up lines, please.)

Sheep show up everywhere in our language: lost sheep, black sheep, good shepherd, fleeced, pull the wool over someone's eyes, led like sheep to the slaughter, spinning a yarn, flocking together, gentle as a lamb, wolf in sheep's clothing, two shakes of a lamb's tail, dyed in the wool, golden fleece, muttonchops, and the leg-o'-mutton sail are just a few examples.

Woolgathering is another one. It isn't used much anymore, but it means to daydream. Yet the word initially meant exactly what it says: to gather wool. In medieval Europe, the wealthy land barons owned both the land and the sheep, but the lower classes were allowed to pick up bits of wool that had snagged on bushes, and spin them up into clothing for their families. Women walked the paths sheep traditionally took, gathering up the tufts. *Wild Fiber* magazine reported that woolgathering was very social, and the women would "frequently stop at farms along the way and perform odd jobs in exchange for food and shelter." Up to four pounds of wool could be gathered from the hedgerow in a single day, and that day began at 4:00 AM. It's hard to understand how a word for lazy daydreaming came from such hard work, but that's the English language for you.

Not only has the use of "woolgathering" almost disappeared in the twenty-first century, but sheep seem to be fading away as well, like photos left too long in the sun. Because the number of sheep in America has fallen 90 percent in the last ninety years, so too has the number of sheep aficionados. But I know they still exist. The shepherds in my sheep producers' group don't talk about how they feel about sheep, so I must look elsewhere. Surely there are other shepherds who have described their love of sheep, so I google "Why I love sheep." Unfortunately, the online people who love sheep have something entirely different in mind, since the first link is for a plastic inflatable, anatomically correct "love sheep" with garter belt and black mesh stockings.

Well. Okay, then. Not exactly what I'd been looking for.

It seems weird, in a world of poverty and environmental degradation and political unrest, to focus so intently on sheep, yet as Anne-Sophie Swetchine wrote, "To love deeply in one direction makes us more loving in all others."

Must you own sheep to be sheepish? I suspect that sheep ownership is not required for unbridled sheepishness. We can *all* love sheep, of course in an entirely healthy and platonic and non-gross sort of way. To be sheepish in an urban setting, all you need is a copy of *Sheep in a Jeep*, a Lamb Chop puppet, and a few wool sweaters. Possessing a wool coat and wool socks bumps you up to the Über-Sheepish class.

To be sheepish in a rural setting, all of the above tools are a fine start, but you should also acquire these five items:

1. Shepherd
2. Sheep
3. A shearer to shear the sheep
4. A market for the wool and meat
5. Lambs

I've somehow woven these elements into a life, but truth be told, I'm not really sure it's the life for me. Hence, a word of caution: The sheepishness experienced after being zapped by an electric fence is temporary. The other sort—of or belonging to sheep, loving them in a healthy and platonic and non-gross sort of way—can be a more permanent condition.

No Snowballs
on This Farm

Only four of my sheep have names. Paula is the
first ewe we bought, and I named her after my
wife . . . I also named both rams. But my favorite ewe actually has no name. She is called
No. 57.

—JON KATZ

Melissa and I are obviously the shepherds. So the next item required for a sheepish life is sheep. Before we even buy the sheep,
however, Melissa and I make a pact. Nicknames for the farmers
are okay, but we will not name our animals. We are determined to
show people we are *not* spending all this money on fifty woolly
pets. We will *not* be those shepherds who bring baby lambs into
the house, strap on disposable diapers, and let them scamper
around like puppies.

We will *not* be those shepherds who name every single sheep in their flock, names like Fluffy and Snowball and Freckles. We are professionals, not hobbyists. Any sheep that learns how to jump the fences, we will sell. Any sheep that doesn't produce twins year after year, we will sell. Any sheep that lacks good mothering skills and refuses to feed her lambs, we will sell. We will be a *real* farm, not a health spa for pampered sheep.

Bad-ass farmers. Hard core farmers. *Real* farmers.

Unfortunately, the first animals we bring home are already named, goats Merlin and Lancelot. We purchase two more goats, these named Ambrosia and Taffy. But we won't name the sheep.

We must name the land, however, since there are no street signs, just sky, soil, and water. If Melissa wants me to help her, I need to know where she is. "Over the hill, past the trees, down the little slope" could be anywhere on the farm. We end up with the cleverly named North Pasture, East Pasture, West Pasture, as well as a few quirkier names, like The Bowl, The T, Madonna Point, The Sacrifice Lot (not what you'd think), and Nacho Hill. But we won't name the sheep.

We finally bring home fifty ewe lambs, each about seven months old, each with a numbered tag in her ear. Those numbers will be their "names": 25, 39, 66. No exceptions. But we also bring two little rams home. As a writer, I own several books of baby names, and before I know it Melissa is poring over the books, and within a few days the rams are Otis and Rudy. Later rams become Andy, Monte, Duncan, Perfect Tommy, Jeffrey, and Erik. So now our rule is: We won't name the *female* sheep.

We purchase llamas to protect our sheep from the coyotes howling in the creek valley all night long, and of course we name each one. First comes Moche, who sadly dies after only two years with us, then the Dynamic Duo: Chachi and Zipper.

A few years later, our friend Mary D. attends the local livestock auction to sell some of her goats, and Melissa accompanies her. Farmers love to watch livestock auctions. Of course I'm always a little nervous when Melissa attends the auction, for there is no telling what she might bring home, but Mary and Melissa return around noon, and all seems well. I feed them lunch. We laugh, we talk, and then Mary must leave.

As she escorts Mary to the door, Melissa gives me a funny look. "Um, I had to borrow $5 from Mary. Do you have enough that I could pay her back?"

I dig into my wallet. "What'd you buy with the $5?"

Mary senses danger. "I have to go home," she says.

"Don't leave until I tell her," Melissa cries.

"Tell me what?" I say sharply, which seems to be happening more lately. "Candy bars?"

"Nope."

"Breakfast?"

"Nope."

Alarm bells clang in my head. The only things you can buy at the livestock market are candy bars, breakfast, and animals.

I jam my fists on my hips. "Goat or sheep?"

"Llama."

Mary leaves in a big hurry and I stomp up to the barn.

Because the crowd at the auction had been small and not that interested in buying, no one bid when a tall, good-looking llama came up for sale.

"$25?" asked the auctioneer. "$20? $15? $10? Do I hear $5?"

Melissa couldn't believe it. A healthy llama and no one wanted him? If she had asked me, I would have said, "The last thing we need on this farm is another llama. We already have two."

She didn't ask me, of course, so instead she borrowed the money from Mary and bought the llama. Someone from the auction trailered the llama to the farm. Melissa and Mary installed the animal in the barn, then came in for lunch without breathing a word of the farm's new resident.

This llama is marked like a pinto pony, white with lots of brown spots. White rings circle both eyes so he looks as if he's wearing goggles. It makes me chuckle.

A llama for $5. Even I can appreciate the value of a good bargain, so household harmony is maintained, especially when I demand naming rights. This is how Tucker comes to live on the farm.

We stick by our "no naming the female sheep" rule. Then Melissa buys two Muscovy ducks, big waddling things that don't quack but sort of whistle in a nonthreatening way. The female proves to be a great mother, so she becomes Mama Duck. The male struts around imperiously waiting for Mama Duck to walk by so he can have sex. I want to name him Oversexed Asshole, but Melissa, being more generous than I am, dubs him Mr. Duck.

I'm having my own struggles with names, since I've realized something about the title of my manuscript about our early farming disasters. "Searching for Placenta by Moonlight" is a terrible title. Because lambing, the time when ewes give birth to their lambs, is difficult for me and because it is the direct result of two sheep engaging in intercourse, I now change the title to "Sheep Sex and Other Natural Disasters." Perfect.

Sadly, while I'm distracted by naming my manuscript, Melissa has entered the Fun House Maze of Naming Animals and can't find her way out. A baby duck Melissa hatches and raises becomes Ping. The next year there's Ping II. Other ducks are Daphne, Helen,

Veronica, and Chloe. The roosters over the years become Serge, Romeo, Sonny, Tony, Dante, and El Guapo. The hens are too numerous for names, but Melissa still knows each one.

I recognize, of course, that not naming our ewes is our feeble attempt to keep our sheepishness in check. Should we begin naming our sheep Snowball or Fluffy, we're goners. I've seen it happen to people made of stronger stuff, so our caution is warranted. We will stick by our guns. We are *not* naming the ewes in our flock. We are bad-ass farmers. Hard core farmers. *Real* farmers.

Tough muffins.

Getting Naked

I think I could sing and shear a few sheep at
the same time.

—ROBERT PLANT

Two shepherds. Fifty sheep. Next? A shearer. Unless the sheep are
hair sheep that shed their fleece like dogs, the sheep will make
wool, lots of it, without any effort at all. Therefore, the sheep must
get naked. Their lambs will find the udders more easily with less
wool in the way. The sheep will be more comfortable in the summer heat.

Every year our shearer, Drew, shows up for our late March shearing day thirty minutes late, with a thermos full of Mountain Dew,
a bottle of Advil, and a plug of tobacco in his cheek. "Did your
mom bring cookies?" When I nod, he starts unloading his truck.
Shearing can be a lonely job. Drew tells of shearing jobs where he
drives onto the farm, the farmer points to the barn—"Sheep'er in

19

there"—then disappears. Drew sets up his equipment by himself, catches a sheep, shears it, stuffs the fleece in the wool bag, sweeps off his shearing board (the piece of plywood he stands on), then catches another one. All day long, all alone.

We, on the other hand, want our shearer to be happy, so we make Shearing Day a party. My mom brings Sloppy Joes, cheese and crackers, and her killer chocolate chip cookies. We have ten to fifteen people there. (Although one year Melissa kept inviting anyone she met, so we had over twenty-five and there was no room to move. That was bad.) We help Drew set up. We catch the sheep and roll them on their rumps to be shorn. We gather up the fleece and bag it.

To get more fleece into the seven-foot-tall wool bag, someone needs to climb into the bag and stomp down the wool. The first bag is usually mine, but then my legs turn to noodles and I happily assign the second bag to someone else. One cool March Saturday a new acquaintance shows up. She stands waiting, trembling with excitement because she really wants to stomp wool. I look her up and down. She has a runner's body, trim and lean. Instead of choosing her, I send someone else up into the bag, then hurry off to deal with another problem. My mom sees the whole thing. "Honey, I'm sorry but you don't weigh enough to pack the wool down." She hands the dejected woman a handful of cookies. "Here, these might help."

We sweep Drew's shearing board. We laugh at his stories and tell a few of our own. Even on a gloomy day, the barn hums with voices, electric clippers, and bleating sheep. Shearing Day is our social event of the year—good friends, faithful family, contagious laughter, and naked sheep.

Our ploy works because Drew keeps coming back, even though shearing on our farm has proven a bit dangerous for him. Other shepherds tease Drew about making sure his health insurance is all in order before coming to our farm.

The first year, after a long day he stepped up onto the metal frame holding the wool bag, slipped, fell back, and hit his head on the frame of the feed room door. Then he just lay there. One woman immediately herded her kids out of the barn because she thought he was dead.

He eventually rose, stubborn as ever, and refused to consider going to the emergency room. It took us thirty minutes to convince him that bleeding profusely from the head wasn't normal. Melissa drove him to the clinic, and they waited hours but a doctor finally got around to closing up that hard head with over twenty stitches.

Not every sheep enjoys being shorn, so now and then one might kick a bit. An article about shearing in *The Shepherd* said shearers need to be "one-part compassion and three-parts gristle." Shearing a 200-pound animal without getting kicked in the groin is a challenge even for the most experienced shearers.

One year, the first sheep Drew sheared was our big ram Monte. Monte disliked being touched by anyone other than a flirtatious ewe in heat, so he kicked Drew hard in the hand. Drew took an Advil, then kept shearing even though the hand swelled up and his fingers grew so stiff he could hardly bend them. I kept asking him if he was okay, if he wanted to stop, but he'd say, "No," then pop some more Advil. He knew if he stopped, his hand would quit working so he sheared all fifty sheep. Then he finally went to the doctor a week later—to learn that Monte had broken his hand. Yet the guy keeps coming back, probably for my mom's chocolate chip cookies.

Technology may be replacing many jobs, but when it comes to sheep, a human shearer is still required. The Aussies tried automatic shearing machines in the late 1980s. The sheep was stretched out with its front and back legs tied, then the automatic clipper moved over its body. In over 1,000 tests very few sheep were injured, but it took a long time to shear one sheep. I found a video on YouTube but couldn't bear to watch it because there are parts of a sheep's body—both male and female—that shouldn't accidentally be sheared off. Thankfully, the automated machine was abandoned as too slow.

A more real threat to a shearing career is the declining number of sheep. In the 1940s, the United States was the fifth-largest producer of wool in the world, but now we produce less than 1 percent. There are 850 million sheep around the planet, so it's not as if they'll become extinct anytime soon, but still, the sheep is fading from view. Even in Australia, where sheep and wool are major industries, numbers have fallen from 200 million in the late twentieth century to just 50 million in 2010. The 2010 International Wool Conference was canceled due to lack of registrations. Sadly, as the number of sheep on the planet fall, more shearers quit because there's nothing for them to shear.

Any sheepish person understands that although you want your accountant, doctor, and dentist to like you, it's not the end of the world if they don't. But because shearers are almost as endangered as sheep, *nothing* is more important than keeping your shearer happy.

Freakishly Exotic People

We are all a little weird and life's a little weird, and when we find someone whose weirdness is compatible with ours, we join up with them and fall in mutual weirdness and call it love.

—AUTHOR UNKNOWN

Because ancient cartographers didn't have the whole picture when constructing maps, they left the undiscovered lands blank. Or they filled in those blanks with fanciful images of what those mysterious lands might hold—"sea serpents, dragons, griffins, hippogriffs, and freakishly exotic people," writes Peter Turchi in *Maps of the Imagination*.

Farms and farming may be one of the blanks on your map, and you've likely filled in the blanks not with sea serpents, but with red barns, black-and-white cows, pink pigs, fluffy sheep, and sturdy farmers who work night and day in the wind and rain and muck and manure. Talk about "freakishly exotic people."

As two of those "exotic" people, Melissa and I must find a market for our products. We find a market for our lamb—people who eat meat and care about how the animals are raised. And just for the record, lamb (the meat) does not come from lambs (the babies), but from animals nearly adult-sized.

We struggle, however, when it comes to a market for the wool. We ship it off to a wholesale wool warehouse, which is what most shepherds do, even if it's not very lucrative. How unlucrative? We recently sent three years' worth of wool to a warehouse in Illinois, where the fleeces were sorted and graded. Based on the grade, we were paid a certain price per pound. Our check came a few months later, and was for $382. By the time we pay the shearer and buy food for the shearing party, our annual expenses are $100, or $300 for the three years. Subtract the $300 in expenses from $382 for a profit of $82, or $27 per year.

Wow. We won't be putting anyone through college on our wool profits. Wool prices have been so low that some smaller farmers just compost the fleece or use it to mulch their gardens.

The other option is to sell the wool directly to those people I'm going to delicately call fiber "fans." As we consider this option, I spend a little time with shepherds who sell their wool to fiber fans. I quickly decide that spinning and knitting and weaving are all major time wasters and I want no part of them. We won't be getting involved in the fiber world. Besides, these people seem a bit loopy and dewy-eyed when it comes to yarn. Not us. We have our feet firmly planted on the ground instead of our heads stuck up in some fleecy sky. But because we produce wool, we now and then brush elbows with spinners, knitters, weavers, people who are, in my opinion, truly freakish and exotic. So when I say fiber "fans," I confess that I really mean "freaks."

A friend, who unfortunately falls into this category, explains her stash. "I love buying yarn, of every color and size, and then I put it in my closet and never get around to knitting it." She laughs. "I can't open my closet." I imagine that if she did, fuzzy skeins of yarn would tumble around her head like dead Tribbles.

A fiber fan will spend hours and hours knitting a wool sock—a *sock*, people—when there are machines out there able to manufacture a perfectly fine pair of wool socks for under $20. There's even a "Sock Summit" with the motto: "Taking Sock Knitting Almost *Too* Far." Forget Extreme Snowboarding, or Extreme Mountain Biking. Recently, when the online registration for this Extreme Knitting event began, 40,000 people tried to register and crashed the system.

In my earlier search for words to describe loving sheep, I came across the British poet Gower, born around 1330. This man had a serious affection for sheep, but an even greater love for wool. Here's what he had to say, speaking directly to his fluffy paramour:

> The beautiful, the white, the delightful one.
> The love of you sings and binds,
> so that the hearts of those who make merchandise of you
> are not able to disengage themselves from you.

Wow. The love of you sings? Gower must have been the original fiber freak. Why someone would be so enamored of wool escapes me, but if I alter Gower's words slightly, they become, "The love of *ewe* sings." This I get.

Fiber fans are so in love with the process that they'll make the same thing over and over again. My friend Kathy and I take the train to Chicago. While I write and read, Kathy knits a pair of fingerless gloves. As the train chugs along, I look over now and then to see her progress. Good, the eight-inch glove is almost done.

Five minutes later there is nothing on her needles but an inch of knitting. "You're on the second glove now?"

"No, I made a mistake and am starting over."

Yikes. A few hours later she has the glove almost done, but then begins unraveling it.

"What are you *doing?*"

"I think I'm going to change the pattern a little," she says calmly as she unravels nearly the entire glove.

"A *little?*" I say weakly. "I'm not sure I can take it if you rip that glove apart a third time."

"Frogging is part of knitting," Kathy says casually.

"Frogging?"

"When you take something apart, you rip it, rip it . . . ribbit, ribbit."

The next week, Melissa and I pull on our rubber barn boots, yank on heavy leather gloves, then head outside to spend two hours pitching straw from the barn floor, straw soaked with cattle piss and caked with manure.

As I tell Melissa about the frogging, and about the "freakishly exotic people" who knit socks, we start pitching wet cow poop.

"Weirdos," we both say.

Spinning in Circles

As long as the world is turning and spinning, we're gonna be dizzy and we're gonna make mistakes.

—MEL BROOKS

If we don't make much money selling to the wholesale wool warehouses, and we feel it's wise to stay as far away as possible from the fiber freaks, what other options do we have? None. It's either one or the other, and we don't like either option. So I decide that perhaps, to better understand the fiber people, I should get more in tune with our wool. I will learn how to spin. I will do so in a grounded way, my level-headedness protecting me from the lure of fiber. So the next year I retain a fleece for myself during our March shearing party. It sits in the feed room for another month until spring arrives and I find the courage to give this a try.

My goals are grand. First I'll clean the fleece, then card it into roving, which means fluffing it. I will spin the roving into yarn, and knit the yarn into something to wear. I buy a spinning wheel and I ask our friend Kim to teach me how to spin.

Kim is someone who can bake a soufflé, starch and iron his dress shirts, knit a pair of Fair Isle gloves, watch TV, and spin. All at the same time. I "iron" by sticking my clothes back into the dryer until the heat removes 50 percent of the wrinkles. In our house, a spinach soufflé looks very much like a frozen pizza. Despite this, we still love Kim.

Spinning's supposed to work like this: Depress a pedal with your foot, the wheel starts spinning, the bobbin turns, the roving pulls from your hand and through a small opening, unfortunately named the orifice, and then around the bobbin. Start the wheel spinning with your hand, then take over with the pedal while your hand gently pinches the roving so it twists and gets sucked through the orifice.

I create my own technique. Start the wheel spinning with your hand, then push the pedal so hard the roving breaks. Stop the wheel, curse softly, then thread the roving back through the orifice, and begin again. I recommend repeating this step approximately twenty-seven times, or until you feel close to tears. On the twenty-eighth attempt you get the speed right and you pinch the roving just right and the yarn begins to twist and accumulate on the bobbin in a mannerly fashion.

Yarn is supposed to be slender, and relatively uniform. Theoretically, one pound of wool can be spun into ten miles of yarn, but not if I'm spinning. Within a space of ten seconds, my yarn goes from the size of my thumb all the way down to dental floss, then back up to thumb-sized. Kim smiles encouragingly and explains this uneven type of yarn, with its slubs and irregularities, is called designer yarn and is highly valued.

Right.

Of course when the yarn is thin dental floss, it breaks, which means I have to stop, rethread it through the little orifice, and repeat my twenty-eight attempts to get the thing spinning again.

Why am I finding this so hard? My mom is creative. My grandmother was the Queen of Crafty. She once sent us a branch cemented into a white mug, the "tree" hung with peanuts. My favorite was her Kewpie doll with the holes poked in its head to convert it into a talcum powder dispenser. Given this background, and given that spinning is a craft, I should be able to conquer it. Millions before me have learned how to spin a plethora of animal and vegetable fibers: alpaca, angora goat, angora rabbit, buffalo, camel, cashmere goat, cat hair, cotton, dog hair, flax, guanaco, hemp, llama, mohair goat, musk ox, ramie, silk, vicuña, wool, and yak.

What's so important about spinning? Abby Franquemont had this to say in *Spin-Off* magazine:

> Without spinning, there is no civilization, no technology, no history, no agriculture, no animal husbandry, no permanent settlements, and the whole of human history just did not happen. Without what I'm doing now, making yarn, there is no life as we know it. Cultures lacking in textile production capability don't generally advance beyond hunting and gathering.

Yes, the iPad's cool, but can it make the same claim? I think not! The first sheep arrived in the American colonies in 1609, and by 1664 Massachusetts alone had over 100,000 sheep. The American colonists were all rabid spinners, determined to free themselves from Britain's expensive cloth. Entire families carried their spinning wheels to church and spun while the minister spoke. Spinning contests were held in the public squares, festivals that attracted huge crowds much as we gather today to watch car derbies or football games or marathons.

The colonies were so serious about spinning that they required it. Massachusetts passed a law requiring each family to spin a pound of yarn a week for thirty weeks out of each year, and the colony charged a penalty of twelve pence for every pound a family fell short. Many families began supporting an unmarried relative or friend in the house to perform the task, which is where the word "spinster" came from.

Even the kids spun. They were so adept that five children under the age of thirteen could spin, weave, and sew all the clothes for thirty people.

To add a rich sheen of irony to all this, my Friend ancestors came to America sometime after the Mayflower but before the Revolutionary War, which makes them American colonists. They surely struggled against the high price of English textiles. They likely spun with the rest of the colonists. The spinning gene must get weaker with every generation, since I obviously haven't inherited it.

Luckily, there are still some people who possess this gene. Among the people who've connected with our farm over the years through my blogs and books is an avid spinner who offers to spin one of our fleeces all the way into yarn. Sure, why not. I'm certainly not getting very far on my own. Sherry is coming to Rochester, so we agree to meet at her hotel. She's in her late fifties, with silver-gray hair and a great smile. Melissa and I shake her hand, then she hugs us both. I take an instant liking to her.

We sit down in the fancy, hushed lobby of the Kahler Hotel. When I open the black plastic bag, the scents of hot wool and lanolin and dried manure float up. "Sorry about the smell," I say.

Without hesitation, Sherry plunges her bare hands into the filthy fleece. "Oh, this is lovely, just lovely. I'm really looking forward to cleaning this up and spinning it." (See what I mean? Fiber freak.) She pulls out handfuls as she continues to praise the fleece, not caring that people are now turning to stare.

Sherry will drag our dirty fleece home with her to Colorado and return in a few months with the finished product. Then I'm contacted by a woman from the East Coast named Karen who loves to dye wool. She offers to turn one of our fleeces into roving, the fluffy stuff spinners use, then dye it. Slightly curious, I send her a box of raw wool, then promptly forget about it. I don't expect much from the fleeces we give to Karen and Sherry, but if these crazy women want to waste—I mean—spend their time this way, fine.

My wheel continues to torture and confound me. I realize I'm not interested enough in the craft to really commit to learning it. Besides, why should I spend a gazillion hours spinning and knitting when I can buy a wool sweater at Macy's for $50? After a few more tries, I tuck the wheel into a corner of our living room and turn it into what Melissa likes to call a Dust Accumulation Research Project. Clearly, our wool market will continue to be the wildly unlucrative wholesale warehouse. I won't be spinning fifty fleeces into yarn anytime soon.

The patron saint of spinners is, interestingly enough, Saint Catherine. She was a Christian martyr in Alexandria. In 307 AD, she was condemned to be torn apart by the spokes of the wheel.

Well. No wonder.

Sheep Sex and
Other Natural Disasters

Lambing, I felt, would take place automatically,
and would be the sheep's business, not mine.

—E. B. WHITE

Shepherds. Sheep. Shearer. Market for wool. Now, for a truly sheepish life, one needs baby sheep.

Starting somewhere mid-May, our ewes paw the ground, turn in circles, and bleat. Then a red bulb of fluid exits each sheep's vagina. Little lamb noses and little lamb toes appear from the same place, and if all goes well, each lamb enters our world with a moist plop onto the ground, followed by a stringy mass of blood and stuff called the placenta.

Lordy. Personally, I'd prefer a stork.

I have no business birthing babies. Unfortunately, I don't know this until I find myself up to my ankles in placentas that first year. If only I'd realized that if you allow a male sheep and a female sheep to have sex, five months later baby lambs will arrive whether you are emotionally ready or not.

As shepherds have done for thousands of years, we let our ewes give birth outside on pasture during warm weather. In the mid-1950s the U.S. Department of Agriculture convinced shepherds it was smarter to bring the sheep into the barn and lamb during the winter as a way to spread out farm tasks. Farmers would have time to lamb because they didn't have any field work. But to do this, farmers must get up several times a night to check on the lambs, for a wet lamb not dried off quickly enough will become hypothermic and die. The barns protect the babies from the snow, wind, and ice, and can be warm inside from all the body heat that the sheep give off. But barns are often damp and moldy, so sheep in barns can get sick, and sometimes being crowded in together interferes with their mothering abilities.

Instead, we time our breeding so the sheep give birth outside in May when it's warm. Instead of being kept in a pen, the ewe chooses her own spot to give birth. She has plenty of room so there are few mothering problems. She knows which lambs are hers and she takes good care of them. We believe so strongly in lambing outside that we only built a three-sided barn, open to the south. Why would we *ever* need a barn for winter lambing?

Our first year of lambing does not go as expected. The farm picks me up and spins me around and around until I'm dizzy. I expect the sheep will give birth one at a time, much as people take numbers at a customer service desk and wait their turn. That four ewes all decide to give birth at the same time seems a really bad idea.

I don't expect them to give birth during rainstorms. I don't imagine that a first-time mother might let one of her lambs nurse, but then get confused and reject the other one, which means I must feed the second lamb with a bottle. I don't expect to come into such intimate contact with so many animal bodily fluids.

I don't expect that a ewe, right in the middle of giving birth, will try to steal another ewe's newborn lamb fifteen feet away, even as her *own* lamb is partially out of the birth canal. I can still close my eyes and see that image. The poor ewe's mothering hormones were so high she couldn't help herself.

Know how irritating backseat drivers are? During lambing I become the most irritating backseat farmer on the planet. "What's happening? Something's going wrong? The lamb's dead! The ewe's going to die! We're all going to die!" I drive us both crazy.

The entire four weeks of lambing is such a shock that after the very last lamb is born, I sit on the front step and cry. We've made it. Lambing is over. Melissa joins me on the steps and tears up as well: "I have to wait an entire *year* before we can do this again." I know opposites attract, but sometimes Melissa and I stretch this theory a bit too far.

Lambing once again happens the following spring, which thrills Melissa and unthrills me. And the third year? Let's just say that my anxiety at lambing is one of the most consistent forces on the planet. After three years it's obvious that the whole birthing thing is considerably outside my comfort zone.

E. B. White wrote, "A lamb, newly born, is in a state of considerable disrepair." He ain't kidding. My fear of lambs in "considerable disrepair" likely sends people into two camps: those who are saddened that I don't find the miracle of birth beautiful and pro-found and deeply moving, and those who, if thrust into the same situation, would prefer to be in the house with me, eating Tostitos and revising Chapter Seven.

Melissa and I both think lambing will get easier for me, but it only gets harder. The more I know what can go wrong, the more I worry.

So when the fourth lambing season rolls around, I get smart. I fire myself.

We find the perfect replacement in Amelia, the teenage daugh-ter of my friend Phyllis. Amelia is between colleges with time on her hands. She is tall, strong, and beautiful, with mischievous eyes and a sparkling smile.

We quickly adjust to life with a teenager in the guest room. She sleeps like the dead, so I need to wake her up the first few morn-ings because Melissa likes to get outside early to check on the flock. That first morning, I stop at the open door, confused. The comforter and top sheet are piled into a lump in the center of the bed. Either Amelia has fled the farm during the night or she is somewhere underneath that pile. I bring Robin the border collie in to stick his cold, wet nose under the mound until it emits a low moan.

"Oh, good," I say. "You're awake. Time to get up."

Amelia is polite. She is funny and makes us laugh, an incredible gift in the midst of high tension. And not once does she say, "I don't want to do that." Instead she constantly asks, "What can I do to help?" She chases sheep, falls down, and picks herself up again. She doesn't complain when the rain starts and doesn't let up for days. Amelia learns to drive the four-wheeler. She learns to set up portable electric fences. And when Melissa thrusts a newborn lamb into her arms and hands her a loaded syringe saying, "Here, you can give the shot," she learns to give shots.

Melissa and Amelia mesh into a team. Soon I rarely have to wake Amelia; she appears at the kitchen counter dressed in her chore clothes even before Melissa is ready. I keep their bellies full and do load after load of laundry, washing off the manure, urine, placenta, dirt, and blood. Both Melissa and I are intensely grateful I can remain in the house. The farm breathes a sigh of relief, and anxiety drops.

I'm not totally out of the picture, however. First with walkie-talkies, then in later years with cell phones, if Melissa or Amelia need anything, they call and I quickly deliver it: more towels, the bottle of propylene glycol, a container for milking out a ewe with teats so full of milk the lambs can't get their mouths around them. If Melissa and Amelia are stuck outside for a long period of time, I deliver water, sandwiches, cookies, and chocolate.

I become the primary audience for stories. Melissa and Amelia might come back in from hours in the rain, excited about saving a baby, or dejected because they haven't. They are overflowing with details, and it's my job to listen and exclaim and con-gratulate, no matter how gory the details or how sad the story's end. So much can happen in one day of lambing that if the stories aren't shared immediately, they're pushed aside by the amazing things that happen the next day. After three days of lambing, what was vivid and intense the first day becomes a dis-tant memory.

Sometimes it's a lamb that has been born overnight and is too weak or cold to stand up and nurse. Melissa often calls ahead be-fore they arrive so I can start thawing the cubes of colostrum we store in the freezer. I put my emotions on hold. The lamb will either survive, or it won't. We'll do our absolute best to make sure it lives, but even then lambs die. I set up a laundry basket in the front entryway with a heating pad covered with a towel. Amelia brings in the lamb and we all sit on the floor gathered around it. If the lamb is strong enough to have a sucking reflex, I can usually get it to drink. If not, Melissa slides a slender rubber tube down its throat, always listening for stomach gases to make sure the tube's in the stomach, not in the lungs; then I pour the colostrum down the tube into the baby's stomach.

Sometimes all it needs is one tubing. A few hours later it drinks from the bottle, or we tube it again. When the lamb is up on its feet and crying, Melissa wraps it in a towel, hands it to Amelia, and they drive back out to the pasture. The ewe is always there waiting, searching for the baby that has disappeared. A bleat from the lamb and a nicker from the ewe bring the two together and the lamb begins to nurse.

One late May morning Amelia zooms up on the four-wheeler and I meet her at the front door. "We can't get the lamb out," she says breathlessly. "We need your help."

"You need my help," I repeat and we look at each other, realizing what a silly request this is. A lamb stuck in the birth canal? A problem that not even Can-Do Melissa and Never-Give-Up Amelia can fix? We're in big trouble.

"You've come to the right person," I say, and I reach for the phone to call the vet. She arrives fifteen minutes later and successfully delivers a huge, coal-black female. I'm proud to play such a critical role in the miracle of birth.

After the first week of Amelia's stay, Phyllis asks Amelia how it's going. "I've never been so exhausted in my life . . . and I've never had so much fun."

I call Phyllis and ask if we can adopt her daughter. We're sad she declines, since after a few weeks with this kid, we're hooked.

The Failed
Environmentalist

It isn't pollution that's harming the environment. It's the impurities in our air and water
that are doing it.

—DAN QUAYLE

I came of age in the 1970s. Earth Day. Recycling. Consume less. Compost. When Melissa and I moved in together, we bought a supply of cloth napkins, and in the nearly thirty years since then I've purchased only a handful of paper napkins. When we moved onto the farm, we built a huge compost bin. We turned off our lights, and minimized our use of both heat and air-conditioning. In fact, for twelve years we didn't even have air-conditioning. We schlepped bottles and newspaper and plastic to recycling centers long before the rest of the world invented curbside pickup.

38

I list all these admirable, eco-friendly activities not to brag, but in hopes that I may be forgiven for what comes next. Thanks to family and health and financial issues, both Melissa and I have been unfocused, overwhelmed, and distracted by all the hats we must wear. But we continue to drive our recyclables into town and put them in the correct bins. The compost pile, however, has grown cold. Instead, we toss some food out in the barnyard for the chickens to munch on, except for the chicken leftovers. That's just not right. The rest of the food scraps find their way into the trash instead of into the countertop compost container. Keeping it clean seems to require more energy than I have.

So I'm feeling a little guilty about the food waste. We should be composting it in a bin of worms under the kitchen sink. But we don't have the time or energy to even look into this. And the job of taking the recycling into town just feels bigger and bigger. It doesn't help that I experiment with drinking a nice big glass of wine every night, so our pantry soon looks alarmingly like the pantry of a person who experiments with drinking a nice big glass of wine every night. And the crushed cans of Diet Coke are piling up and threatening a coup of the kitchen.

Recycling suddenly feels futile and exhausting. Then, with all the stress and crankiness and messiness of life, it happens. One day, as I contemplate filling the car with twenty bags of catalogs and magazines to recycle, five bags of newspapers, three large trash bags with glass, plastic, and aluminum, I crack. Melissa isn't home, so she doesn't see me throw all the recycling into our huge trash bin, which will be emptied that afternoon.

I collapse in the house, feeling so relieved. Once the relief fades, however, the guilt settles in for a nice long visit. Melissa comes home and sees the house unencumbered by 500 pounds of recyclables. "Hey, thanks for taking in the recycling."

How shall I answer? I check my watch. Will the trash guys be here soon? Can I stall? If I tell Melissa the truth, will she march out to the trash bin and remove it all? Is failing to answer a question the same as telling a lie?

The floor beneath us shakes a bit. The trash guys are coming down the driveway in their massive truck. I look Melissa in the eye and she reads the truth. "You didn't."

"I did." I attempt to justify my actions, but her disapproval is impenetrable.

I am a failed environmentalist. It's not just recycling. I hate the new light bulbs. They protrude from light fixtures and bug me. In my opinion, compact fluorescent light bulbs work just fine unless you actually need to see. I can't read with these bulbs. I can't see with these bulbs. The basement stairs go from well-lit and safe to a dim, depressing tunnel. Every time Melissa installs one, I curse and whine and say environmentally inappropriate things, then I remove the offending bulb and screw an incandescent bulb back in.

Should incandescent bulbs ever be outlawed, I envision a Waco-type standoff, with me barricaded inside the house, and U.S. marshals circling outside, guns drawn. They'll hand Melissa the bullhorn so she can plead with me to give myself up before anyone gets hurt. When this doesn't work, a marshal will take over. "Come out with your hands full of those incandescents, or we're coming in."

Given my failed environmentalism, I am relieved we're at least raising sheep on pasture. Grazing animals is much more environmentally friendly than sticking them in a feedlot and using lots of

fossil fuel to plant a crop of grain, spray the crop with herbicides
and insecticides, harvest the grain, dry the grain, transport the
grain to the feedlot, and feed it to livestock. With grazing, the
animals do all the work. They eat, they fertilize. Then they walk
to a new area of the pasture. They eat, they fertilize. It's a beautiful
system.

But then I receive disturbing news. While researching a book I
learn that in 2006, the UN published a report called "Livestock's
Long Shadow" that identified meat production as responsible for
18 percent of all greenhouse gas emissions on the planet, much
more than the entire transportation sector of the world economy.
What? It's more damaging to the environment to eat a hamburger
than to drive a car? How could this be? Said Henning Steinfeld, se-
nior author of the report: "Livestock are one of the most significant
contributors to today's most serious environmental problems. Ur-
gent action is required to remedy the situation." The report goes
on (and on and on) to list all the horrible ways livestock are really
messing things up. The report leads to catchy news headlines like,
"Cattle, Pigs, and Sheep: Environment's Worst Enemies?" The
anti-meat campaigns jump on this, and soon even Prince Charles
is recommending we stop eating meat altogether to save the planet.

There is no response debunking the study, only more and more
organizations enthusiastically quoting it. People in the meat industry are fairly silent, basically because they're already being harassed,
as well they should be, for raising animals in energy-intensive factories. No one seems to be distinguishing between raising livestock
in factories versus raising them out on pasture. The report has
effectively put a red circle with a slash squarely over livestock of
any kind, including my innocent little sheep living quietly out on
our pasture.

What about all the benefits to grazing animals? What counts, environmentally, is not only our emissions, but as *Newsweek* put it, "how the earth responds" to our actions. Half of the carbon we release into the atmosphere is absorbed, much of it by plants that suck it up through photosynthesis. It's a cool cycle, actually—the more carbon dioxide in the air, the more the plants take up so the faster they grow to absorb even more carbon. Plants are good, in other words. It's a reason to keep as much land in pasture as possible.

But no one says this. Instead, the outcry is loud: Livestock are bad for the environment. I don't believe it. But yet, what if it's true?

Great. I throw away my recycling. I don't compost. I use incandescent bulbs. And I raise sheep.

The planet is doomed, and it's my fault.

Minnesota Cranky

I hate to advocate drugs, alcohol, violence, or
insanity to anyone, but they've always worked
for me.

—HUNTER S. THOMPSON

Even though I have referred to myself as a tough muffin, I must
now be brutally honest: I have never been even remotely tough. I
was born shy and became a properly polite child. I hated drawing
attention to myself. The first time Melissa and I went grocery shop-
ping together I was at one end of the cereal aisle and she, from the
other end of the very long aisle, actually called out to me, "Regular
or Honey Nut?" Mortified, I hustled down the aisle. "Please don't
do that," I whispered.

"Do what?"

"Don't talk to me . . . you know . . . so loudly. People will hear."

The poor woman looked around. "You're embarrassed if people know you prefer regular over Honey Nut?"

Add to this shyness the pressure to be "Minnesota Nice," and you have someone who doesn't want to rock the boat or draw attention to herself or do anything that might lead total strangers to think poorly of her.

But something is happening to me and it feels weird.

The first time I realize my personality is getting wonky is when I'm driving 70 mph on Interstate 94 through Wisconsin. There is no traffic behind me. But suddenly, out of nowhere, a motorcycle passes me. He must be going 90 mph to have come up on me so quickly. Speeding pisses me off. Being startled pisses me off. When he passes me, my middle finger goes up before my brain can stop it. Only then do I see the back of his black leather jacket: "Hells Angels, Madison, Wisconsin."

If you know anything about Madison, Wisconsin, you know this isn't as frightening as it sounds. Madison is a college town, a liberal city where every window seems to display a peace sign. Now if the jacket had read *Milwaukee,* Wisconsin, I might have been a little worried. Tougher city. Blue collar. Home of Old Milwaukee beer.

The cyclist gets about fifty feet past me when it sinks in that I've flipped him off. He touches his brakes and drops back, level with me. I'm still too angry to worry about this guy being a Hells Angel. I glare at him from my righteous perch and wave my cell phone at him, then start talking into it, as if I'm tattling on him. The guy guns his bike and disappears on the horizon. See what I mean about Madison?

Meanwhile, Melissa is in the passenger seat staring at me. "Who *are* you?"

Good question. It's like I've reached some weird place in my life where I don't care what other people think of me. Then another day I'm once again in my car, this time on Highway 52, just beginning to pass a man who's driving slowly in the left lane. He has his phone on the steering wheel and he's texting. I am furious. He could cause an accident and someone could die. I pull up next to him. I can't yell because he won't hear me. I'm so frustrated. What can I do?

When the driver looks over at me, I whip out my index finger and shake it at him in furious indignation. Shake, shake, shake, like he's four years old. The guy's eyes widen and he pulls ahead to escape Crazy Woman. I keep shaking my finger and he watches me, alarmed, in his rearview mirror.

My reign of terror continues. We live on a dead-end gravel road in the country, so people driving on the highway often pull off onto our road to nap, make a phone call, or consult a map. I have no problems with this. One summer afternoon as I'm going into town to run errands, I see a car pulled over on our road. The driver, a young man in his thirties, is walking around the front of the car and into the ditch, reaching for his zipper. This stretch of highway has a gas station every ten minutes. It's not a barren wilderness with hours between public toilets.

He's chosen a spot without bushes or trees. Cars whiz by 100 feet from him. There's a house directly across the highway. The grass is short, but I doubt this guy is planning to kneel. He stops in the ditch, sees me come over the hill, but keeps going with the zipper. Unbelievable. Can't you be arrested for this in the city?

I am incensed. Using my angry index finger, I blast my horn all the way down the hill. He stops, obviously deciding to wait until I pass, but clearly still planning to pee. I am even more incensed, so when I reach him I slam on my brakes and roll down the win-dow. "This neighborhood is *not* your toilet!" I scream, scaring even myself. "Go pee somewhere else!"

He flings up his hands and stomps back to his car. I drive away, shaken but exhilarated. Some days, dropping the Minnesota Nice feels pretty good.

I share my confrontational stories with my dad. He frowns. "Where did you get that from? Not from me. Not from your mother." Realization dawns. "Ah, from your mother's mother. Your Grandma LaRiviere could be . . ." He searches for a delicate way to phrase this, then gives up. "Your grandmother could be ornery."

My grandmother raised sheep. I raise sheep. My grandmother could be "ornery." I was turning ornery.

Hmmm.

The King and I

The Lord can give, and the Lord can take away.
I might be herding sheep next year.

—ELVIS PRESLEY

I like Elvis. I like his R&B songs. I like his voice. And I think he was physically a beautiful man. I try to convince Melissa to name our latest ram "Elvis," but she won't. I begin sharing my love of Elvis with friends. That's all they hear when they ride in my car. I have photos of him in my office. I can tell by their concerned faces that if I don't move on soon, there will be a well-meant intervention in my future.

My dad and stepmother visit Graceland, and since I've never been, I ask Dad to bring me something back. He buys me a book about Elvis's life, complete with photos of Graceland. I spend one entire morning reading the book, mesmerized by his strange and complex life. When I'm done, I close the cover and begin to cry.

I cry for thirty minutes. Why? Because Elvis is dead. Yes, he died in 1977, but only now, over thirty years later, does it hit me. The loss is overwhelming.

Six months later I burst into tears again. Elvis is still dead. And again three months after that. Melissa grows concerned. Not only have I become Crazy Woman on the road, but I can't stop crying over Elvis.

I've already had my midlife crisis, so I'm not sure what's going on now. When I was forty, and flailing around as a writer and new farmer, I pushed through and found myself on the other side of a few really bad years. To celebrate, I got a six-inch tattoo of a mermaid on my back. I was so relieved to have moved through this phase in my life that for weeks I'd pull my clothing aside to show off my tattoo. Melissa finally suggested, gently, that I stop disrobing in public. I decided that when I do weird things like showing off a tattoo, it means I've survived something.

So if I've already had my crisis, why am I crying so much, as if I'm stuck in a PMS loop? I grow concerned about my constant crying, so I make an appointment to see a therapist. In our first session, she asks for examples.

"Well, don't laugh," I say, "but I burst into tears fairly regularly because Elvis is dead."

She laughs. Then she prescribes antidepressants, which I take for a while but since I continue to cry over Elvis, I decide they aren't working and stop. Besides, even though I know I shouldn't like Crying-over-Elvis-Woman, or Crazy-Behind-the-Wheel-Woman, I do. I have great affection for my deteriorating personality. It's like every vertebra in my spine has gone from mush to metal.

I like it.

Brokeback Farm

After you've done a thing the same way for two
years, look it over carefully. After five years,
look at it with suspicion. And after ten years,
throw it away and start all over.

—ALFRED EDWARD PERLMAN,
NEW YORK TIMES, JULY 3, 1958

Because pasture is scarce one fall, Melissa sets up the temporary
netting outside the main fence to let the sheep munch on grass
and clover in the windbreak. They are still fenced, only not with
a heavy-duty perimeter fence. Our flock has never been outside of
the fences because we live an alarmingly short jog to a major highway, and it isn't safe.

The next day, Melissa leaves for work and all is well. Mid-
morning, I look out an east window and see there are sheep in the

49

backyard. This isn't right. I look out the west window. There are sheep on the driveway. Also not right.

Then it hits me. The entire flock is *outside* our perimeter fence. They are unfenced. They are fence free. They have the unfettered ability to dash down into the neighbor's alfalfa field and gorge themselves so badly they bloat up and die. Or they can run down the driveway and turn left, where they can perform all sorts of mischief on a neighbor's land. Or they can turn right, and in a comfortable ninety-second dash find themselves at the highway, where they'll face death by speeding car.

My heart nearly stops when I realize it's up to me to get the flock back to safety. I throw the puppy in her kennel, jam my feet into my barn Birkenstocks, then race outside. Our border collie, Robin, is now mostly deaf, so he can no longer help, and there's no time to call a neighbor because as the sheep graze, they are spreading out farther from the house.

I dash to the barn for a bucket of corn, then race for the fence that should have kept them in. They knocked it down. I disconnect the electricity so I can touch the fence, then run to the pasture where I need to move them.

I'm a planner. I consider the options, weigh the results, and then make a decision. This time I act on pure instinct. The sheep are outside the temporary fence, but the llamas are still inside. When I open the fence to call the sheep in, the llamas will want to leave. They are contrarians like you wouldn't believe. I decide I'd rather have three llamas running loose than the entire flock.

I have one chance to lure them down the driveway into a ninety-degree right turn, up the hill, then a ninety-degree left turn into the pasture. If this doesn't work, they'll become suspicious, flighty, and will likely run in one woolly mass down the driveway.

I open the fence, rattle the bucket of corn, give the odd yodel we use to call the flock, and all the sheep come running from the yard, driveway, and barnyard. A handful make the ninety-degree turn and start following me. The rest hesitate. As I expected, the llamas head for the opening and freedom. In a burst of energy fueled by terror, I push up the hill, rattling the bucket and yodeling. I risk a peek over my shoulder. Thank God for the sheep's desire to stick together. They all make the turn and follow me up the hill. Even the llamas come, having been swept up in the woolly crowd.

I turn left into the pasture, and every sheep and llama follows me. I shut the gate behind them, fall to my knees, and mourn Elvis. If there's a god or goddess or saint responsible for watching over shepherds, he or she has smiled on me today. There are many things on the farm at which I am of no use, but I am a shepherd, and I know how to move sheep. I don't know if my shepherd grandmother even liked sheep, so she might have thought I was wacko to be raising them, but still, I wish she could have seen me today.

After staggering to my feet, I turn to face the naughty sheep, fling my arms wide, and in what comes dangerously close to a bad parody of *Brokeback Mountain*, shout, "I wish I could quit you!" A few sheep look up, bits of grass sticking out of their mouths as they chew thoughtfully.

I love these animals. There's No. 66, still going strong. There's No. 75/101. Her baby ear tag was No. 75, and because she was raised as a bottle lamb, she learned her number. But when we gave her an adult tag, No. 101, she didn't know we were calling her. So she became No. 75/101. Sounds like a radio station when we call out her name . . . I mean, her number. We don't name our sheep.

I watch No. 75/101 return to her grazing after my outburst.

Despite my sheepishness, I might be a bit cranky to still be farming. I've barely made a dent in all the places I'd hoped to visit. I imagine that other people are having considerably more fun in their lives than I'm having in mine. They're dressing better, earning more, and are just more together than I am. They're going to more parties, attending more plays and movies, taking interesting classes. Their smart phones live more interesting lives than I do. I need a break.

So where can a farmer escape when she's tired of farming?

It's a quiet afternoon and we're both inside. I sit at my computer in my office, and outside my open door Melissa sits at her desk in the family room. Suddenly Melissa leaps from her desk and heads for the stairs. "Something's wrong," she cries. "A sheep's in trouble."

I wince, *totally* busted by the sheep bleat that Melissa has just heard. "No, that's not a real sheep."

She stops on the stairs. "Not a real sheep."

I sigh. "It's a virtual sheep."

She now stands in my office looking over my shoulder at my computer screen. "What the hell are you doing?"

I purse my lips, wishing I'd thought to mute the animal sounds on the game. "I'm playing FarmVille."

She looks at me as if I've lost my mind, which isn't far off.

I'd first learned of the game through a *New York Times* article. Apparently FarmVille could be played through Facebook. By the end of 2009, the game's first year, over 62 million people signed up to play. This means that the number of virtual Farmville farmers outnumbered *actual* farmers by more than sixty to one.

In FarmVille, you're given land and seeds to plant, then once your "crop" has matured, you harvest and sell it. While you "farm," pleasant music plays in the background, punctuated now and then by a cow mooing or a sheep bleating.

From the article, it seemed life as a virtual farmer went like this: Check your computer every day. When your harvest time nears, set your alarm before going to bed. Wake up when alarm sounds. Turn on light. Reach for laptop. With a click, harvest your blueberries and put them up for "sale." Turn out light. Go back to sleep.

I'm not sure if this game is good or bad. Do virtual chores help people better appreciate the work involved in raising real blueberries? Or does the game increase the sense that food appears on the shelf without much effort?

I decide that rather than criticize a game I've never played, I should give it a try. I sign up and my farm appears with six little brown plots in an acre of green. I plow those six plots, then plant them with strawberries. I return a few days later to find that my strawberries have withered and died. They matured but I hadn't harvested them in time.

A day later when I move my cursor over my cow, it says "97% complete." This must mean the cow is 97 percent on her way to needing to be milked. What I don't know is how long it will take for that last 3 percent to happen. And when she reaches 100 percent, what if I don't milk her right away? Will I log onto the game to find the cow belly up?

It's my day to do real chores on our real farm, but I find it hard to concentrate. As I fill the sheep waterer, I worry about my virtual cow. As I make sure the steers have fresh water, I worry about my virtual cow.

Barely noticing the warm summer day or the live animals around me, I finish chores and race inside. The cow is "100% complete" but hasn't exploded or died, so I "milk" it, sighing with relief. Then I happily plant some "strawberries" and feed the "chickens."

I start playing every day, then twice a day. I accumulate a flock of sheep. I build fences, but in a funny little twist, I leave an opening in the fence, my own way of making the virtual farm more real. And sure enough, the next time I log on, two sheep have escaped the pasture and are in the strawberries. I scold them affectionately and move them back. It's a very different experience than those ten minutes of terror as I worked to get fifty real sheep back inside the real fence.

Virtual farming is fun. It's clean. There are no disasters.

When it comes to real farming, there are days when I think: Okay, enough is enough. We've done this for fifteen years. Fifteen years of little travel, not much money, and a great deal of manure on my jeans. We recently purchased four baby calves, and as I carried one into the barn, he peed all the way through to my underwear.

An idea takes root in the back of my mind. What if we sell the house and the farm, then buy a small, cute RV? We could travel around the country picking up odd jobs. We'd have fewer headaches, fewer expenses, fewer urine-soaked pairs of underwear. It would be new. It would be less stressful. It wouldn't be farming.

Searching for
Memoirs by Moonlight

Perhaps, being lost, one should get loster.

—SAUL BELLOW

Perhaps, being lost, one should get lobster.

—DEAN YOUNG

I continue to struggle with the name of my book about the farm. Then the scandal breaks about James Frey and his novelized memoir, *A Million Little Pieces*. He was a bit too free with the truth in his book, and Oprah smacked him down for it. When I worry that as a result, people will no longer believe memoirs, Melissa snorts and says I could always call my memoir "A Million Little Fleeces." No wonder I love this woman.

I find an agent who's willing to sell "Sheep Sex and Other Natural Disasters." It takes her a few years, during which time I work as an instructor for a correspondence course, and continue raising sheep, but the agent finds an editor who loves the manuscript. The only problem, the editor says, is the book's name. Apparently the phrase "sheep sex" might take people's minds in the wrong direction. Uff da.

So I once again rename the book, this time *Hit by a Farm: How I Learned to Stop Worrying and Love the Barn*. The one surprising thing about the book's publication is that both farmers and farming enthusiasts come out of the woodwork. Farmers approach me at speaking engagements, look around to make sure no one else can hear, then confess they had the same accident with the drag as Melissa did, or that they'd also let their tractor run out of oil. Sadly, no one confessed to planting 200 grapevines upside down.

Gay and lesbian farmers reach out to me. I meet elderly people who love the book because it brings back memories of growing up on a farm. I meet middle-aged people who speak wistfully of having wanted to farm at one time in their lives. I meet young men and women who rush up to me and say, "I've always wanted to farm, and after reading your book, I want to farm even more."

I gently suggest to each of them that they should reread the book, repeatedly, until their sanity returns.

The weird thing about publishing a memoir is that the characters in it are frozen in time, like little action figures perfectly preserved in amber. Melissa and I are in our late thirties when we begin the farm. *Hit by a Farm* is published ten years later. During dinner with friends, I meet a man who has just read my memoir. In his mind, I must be forever energetic, forever earnest, forever thirty-seven. As I shake the man's hand, the words slip out before he can censor himself: "Wow. You have more of a patina than I'd imagined."

Patina. A sheen produced by age or wear.

Gee, thanks.

In reading the book, people have laughed with us and learned with us and shared our story with others. There's the lesbian in Puerto Rico who felt estranged from her mother, judged because of her sexuality. She gave her our story to read. I'm not sure what actually went through the mother's mind—recognizing that being a shepherd was weirder than being gay? Relief her daughter didn't raise sheep? Either way, upon finishing the book the mother invited her daughter and partner out for dinner, and the relationship began to mend.

Others find in the book encouragement that their relationships will survive the start of a new venture or project. Some use it as a manual on how to raise sheep. People love that two women started a farm and have stuck with it. The praise embarrassed us: "You two are amazing!" "Look what you've done! You've started a farm! You're living your dream!" Over the years, nonfarmers repeatedly reach out and lightly touch our lives as if to reassure themselves we're still here, still together, as if they're emotionally invested in our ongoing success. If we continue farming, it seems to give people hope for making changes in their own lives. One reader wrote, "I love the way you two found your way out of the misery and into the sunshine again." Another said, "I'm glad you found the balance that makes your lives work."

Sigh. How did two introverted shepherds become role models for farming, healthy relationships, and balance? If people are relying on me to show them the way, they're in big trouble . . .

basically because I've begun turning to memoirs myself in search of direction and encouragement. Just as Melissa and I aren't preserved in amber at age thirty-seven, neither is the farm, and neither is our relationship. We're slogging through both. And as for balance in my life? My muse took that with her when she left.

I'm not thirty-seven anymore. I'm confused about what I want and where I'm going. I want to know if sheep are ultimately fatal to a relationship.

One day I tiptoe right up to the edge of the abyss. I ask Melissa, "What do you suppose would happen if we sold the farm?" Her eyebrows totally disappear into her hairline. "Just kidding," I say with a jolly laugh. I'm not interested in totally gutting Melissa's life. Forget I mentioned it.

I start cruising memoirs. There are travel and spiritual memoirs. I was hoping for one entitled, "Eat Pasture-Raised Lamb, Pray for Less Chaos, and Love Your Sheep." No such book to be found. There are food and wine memoirs, but because our pantry still looks like a bottle recycling center, perhaps not. The "I will survive" memoirs deal with serious illness, pain, and death. I'm not ready for that yet.

There are now a flock of "farm" memoirs about being enslaved by ducks or singing the praises of goats or loving llamas, about moving to the country and giving agriculture a try. Most of these farm memoirs deal with the farm's beginning because that's the most fun—things go wrong, the "farmers" make fools of themselves, people plant grapevines upside down. (Well, okay, that was just me.)

Nowadays, new farmers not only write memoirs but star in their own reality shows like "The Fabulous Beekman Boys." Josh Kilmer-Purcell and Brent Ridge, together for ten years, buy a huge

New York farm that comes with a mansion, a herd of goats, and its own farmer. Brent's upset because the tractors (plural—they need more than one?) aren't neatly lined up in a row. Josh is upset because Brent is making him work too hard. Funny stuff. A *Salon* article trumpets the story of Josh and Brent: *Can farming cure a midlife crisis?* Of course it can't, and the article comes to this conclusion: Even if you're farming, your life still holds all the irritating things you want to escape—personality flaws, ego, financial woes. My advice to Josh and Brent? Don't expect a farm to fix your life, for once the rural romance dims, you must still muck out the barn and stack hay bales and give that sick goat an enema. I'm guessing farming causes more crises than it cures.

Farm beginnings are funny, which is why people write about them and watch TV shows about them. The middles of farms? Less hysterical. Hopefully, a farmer gets better at what she does. (If not, that's just sad.) She makes fewer mistakes, creates fewer disasters, and this is good. Although there are tons of stories about starting something new, there just aren't that many about how to *keep* doing something, about how to slog through the middle when the going gets tough.

Also, it seems that in any memoir I pick up that purports to be about one thing—moving to a large city, being laid off—there's always a major relationship breakup buried in the middle of the book. Oddly, as if divorce were a spectator sport, some writers feel compelled to write about their breakups. Frankly, I'm more interested in avoiding my own.

So while I tip my hat to the Beekman Boys, and all the other people fleeing the city and getting into farming, that's not where I am. I suspect my raw truth is one we all face: Barring the sudden publication of a memoir written by another sheepish woman with patina, I must find my own way through the forest by weaving together the stuff of my life.

Weaving requires two threads to create fabric. The vertical threads are called the warp. These threads must be the strongest because they bear most of the stress. My warp threads are farm stories. Stories, both good and bad, are the reason that people not only start farming, but *keep* farming.

The horizontal threads of woven fabric are called the weft, or woof. Since I love dogs, let's go with woof. These threads can be more fragile, but they create the fabric—its color and design. My woof threads are sheep and fiber stories, threads that will prove stronger than I'd imagined.

PART

TWO

Telling Farm Tales

To Sproing and Worfl

Jumping for joy is good exercise.
—AUTHOR UNKNOWN

Our farm has had its ups and downs, but I believe that it's lasted fifteen years because of the thread of joy that runs through those farms where the animals are happy, calm, and contented. You can't be around such animals without absorbing a bit of their zen.

Despite my current confusion over what I want to be when I grow up, without sheep in my life I would greatly miss the joy. Two of the most blatant animal joy indicators on a farm are sproings and worfls.

Animals jump, leap, and spring, but they also sproing. If you've ever watched cartoons, you've likely seen an animal sproing, but few nonfarmers have been lucky enough to see an actual sproing-ing. When an animal sproings, all four legs leave the ground at the same time and the animal bounces *way* up into the air. An animal will often sproing when it's excited—wheee! Or if it's the last one through the gate, it might sproing to confuse me in case I'm a wolf.

Four legs up, four legs down, four legs up. It's one of the most surprising things you'll ever see an animal do. Talk about defying gravity. Many marketing campaigns use the tired, worn out "Think Spring!" A truly innovative marketer would switch to "Think Sproing!"

Our llamas have a job to do—protecting the sheep from predators—but Melissa also expects them to cooperate when we're moving sheep. She will often explain to the llamas where she wants the sheep to go and ask the llamas to help. Sometimes the llamas lead the sheep right up to the correct gate. Other times the llamas turn their backs on her and become the French guy up in the castle in *Monty Python and the Holy Grail*—"I fart in your general direction."

Although we can't physically touch the llamas very often because they don't like that, they do allow us to admire them. One spring afternoon when Melissa and I are working in the West Pasture, she grabs my arm. "Look!" I whirl around to see Chachi not walking, not running, but *sproinging* across the grass. Sproinging lambs are adorable, but when a 450-pound llama sproings, his legs tuck up under his body, his fleece lifts like a curtain, and it seems like a scientific miracle.

The second thing that happens on a sheep farm is worfling. A worfl is a sound I've heard for fifteen years but didn't know there was a word for it until I found it on a farmer's Web site. It may not be a widely accepted term—perhaps this shepherd merely adopted it on her own—but *worfl* deserves to be more widely used. It's a great word.

When a ewe is in labor, she'll bleat loudly because it hurts, damn it, but she'll also, now and then, nicker softly in her throat.

When the lamb is born and only seconds old, as the ewe is licking off the lamb she makes the same throaty, deeply contented sound. It's a sound that's unique to her, a sound that the lamb will recognize among a chorus of other ewes. That sound is worfling.

I've only found a few other uses for "worfl." Someone tweeted that her dog was happily worfling in his sleep. Another spoke of people worfling over the toffee-flavored coffee at the office.

People also sproing and worfl. I used to run through the pasture in pursuit of a wayward lamb. I'd throw myself on the ground to catch a sheep, albeit not as enthusiastically as Melissa, but I took my share of spills. Yet one recent day when Melissa lunges for a sheep and snags its back leg but can't reel the kicking animal in close enough to examine a cyst on its freshly shorn back, I just stand there.

Do I fling myself across the sheep to control its struggling?

No.

Do I drop to my knees and press the ewe up against the barn wall?

Sadly, no.

"A little help here?" Melissa asks as she wrestles in the straw with the ewe.

I just stand there. This is not one of my prouder farming moments.

When did this hesitation to throw myself on the ground start? I don't like it. I begin hesitating at every turn. Will I hurt tomorrow if I do this? Could some part of me be bruised, broken, or dismembered if I proceed with this activity?

Melissa conquers the ewe herself out of sheer determination, then deals with the abscess (details of this procedure aren't really necessary as they will interfere with digestion). But she needs help getting up after she's let the ewe go. She winces as she stretches out her hip and rolls the tension from her shoulders. The next day a colorful bruise appears across her thigh.

It's hard for me to imagine, but could it be that I no longer sproing? Could it be that Melissa doesn't sproing as often, or as high, as she used to? We still worfl, but that's not hard on the knees.

They say memory is the first thing to go, but really, it might be the sproing. Luckily, our animals still sproing, so this joy might be the strongest thread running through the warp.

The First
Pasture Goddess

We experience moments absolutely free from
worry. These brief respites are called panic.

—CULLEN HIGHTOWER

A lamb is born in a large pasture, a tiny speck of white in an
ocean of green. Melissa and I hop on the four-wheeler and approach the new life. Amelia will be here in a few days, not soon
enough for either me or Melissa.

Me: "What if the mother leaves? What if she abandons the
lamb?"

Melissa: "Just relax. The mom isn't going anywhere." Even after years of doing this, I am doubtful, but the ewe does remain in
the same place, only drifting ten feet away to graze.

Another day we find a confusing situation in the pasture. Three lambs stand together, with two ewes beside them crying for their babies. The newborn lambs stagger around in confusion.

Me: "What's going on? The ewes don't know which babies are theirs. This is a disaster. We're going to have to bottle feed all three."

Melissa: "Just relax. We'll find the placentas and figure it out." We walk the area until we find all three placentas in the grass. Like a detective, Melissa pieces together the truth, based on the number, location, and freshness of the placentas. We sort the families out for a happy ending.

After a lamb is born, we must steal it from its mother for about ten minutes to do things to it. Call it processing, or call it welcoming. We sneak up on a pair of sleeping twins and each pick one up. The ewe no longer sees her babies on the ground and panics.

Me: "The ewe is leaving! She's running back to the flock. She's abandoning her babies!" These statements are based not on fear but on the fact that the bleating ewe has run back to the flock, thus abandoning her babies.

Melissa: "Just relax. She'll come back."

Melissa holds her lamb up, looks it in the eye and says, "Hey, you're new here, aren't you? I haven't seen you before." She might stop there, or she might try a few more, including her favorite, "So, you work? Go to school?" while the lamb gazes back, a trifle confused at the rapid-fire pick-up lines. I'm snickering in the background even though I've heard all the lines before. I am easily entertained.

Melissa's right. The lamb's mother comes back. She stands right beside me and bellows into my ear while Melissa works. Introductions out of the way, Melissa gives the lamb a vitamin shot.

She dips its navel in iodine to protect against disease. Then she gives it a numbered ear tag, since we need to know who belongs to whom.

The ear tag number is fine when the animal's in your arms, but as a lamb is streaking by at 100 mph, reading the two-inch tag can be a bit of a challenge. So Melissa developed a lamb decorating system, using waxy sticks made for marking a sheep.

If the lamb is a single, it gets a single stripe across its back, from side to side. If they're twins, each gets two stripes, and the color scheme varies for each set: red-yellow, red-black, and so forth. These color combinations are coded to the ewes, so we can keep track of families. Thank goodness we have few quadruplets born, since those little backs don't have room for four wide stripes.

So if Melissa sees a sick lamb fifty feet away, she knows by the green-black-yellow stripes that it's a triplet belonging to Ewe No. 101. One year we had nearly 150 lambs born so Melissa ran out of color combinations and got so creative with crosshatching that the lambs looked like football fans wearing their favorite team colors.

Next, Melissa slips a tight green rubber band over the tail, which will cut off the blood supply. The tail will atrophy and drop off after two weeks or so. As beginning farmers, we castrated the males with a nasty tool called an emasculator. It wasn't Melissa's favorite procedure, so we switched to banding, sliding the green bands onto the base of the scrotum. It worked the same way as with the tail.

After a few years of this, however, Melissa reads that lambs grow faster if you leave their testicles intact. So we start leaving off the bands. All we have to do is make sure that we separate these ram lambs in the fall, when each sheep's thoughts turn to sex. This decision, unfortunately, will return to haunt us in the future.

By the time Melissa finishes "welcoming" the lambs, I've gone deaf, thanks to the ewe yelling in my ear. We kiss each lamb on the head, then return them to the ewe and the yelling stops.

Although I might worry a bit more than necessary, there *are* real reasons to worry. You just never know what's going to happen out on that pasture. We're plagued with what's called a thirteen-striped ground squirrel, basically a skinny gopher that loves to make tunnels in our vineyard and leave little holes everywhere. The best way to get rid of gophers is to have a badger come visit. And about once a year a badger moves into the vineyard. We've never seen him, but in his enthusiasm for gettin' a gopher lunch, he leaves massive holes, holes the riding lawn mower can disappear into if I'm not careful.

The badger doesn't limit himself to the vineyard. He occasionally follows the gophers into the pasture, leaving gaping holes that Melissa must fill so the animals don't break their legs. In one pasture there's a hole so deep that when she moves the sheep there, she rolls the mineral feeder directly over the hole to protect the sheep. (The mineral feeder is a bin mounted on sort of a metal hula hoop so it can be easily rolled from place to place.) The next morning when she rolls the mineral feeder away, two little faces look up at her. Two baby lambs have somehow gotten themselves stuck in the hole. Their wide ears are a bit soiled, but otherwise the lambs are fine. Melissa gently pulls each lamb from the hole and they scamper off.

See? What if Melissa hadn't found those lambs until a few days later? It's hard not to worry. Thankfully, Amelia finally arrives. The worry wart stays in the house, and Amelia does her thing. Her competence grows every year. Her sheep senses sharpen. One day Amelia and Melissa move the entire flock from the Tree Pasture near the noisy highway into the first section of the North Pasture. Later, as they're preparing to leave, Amelia thinks she hears something back in the trees. She searches the large grove, stepping over logs and avoiding low-hanging branches until she comes face-to-face with a little lamb, all alone. He was probably sound asleep when the sheep left, woke up and had no idea where his mom had gone.

Amelia snags the little guy and carries him back to his mother, who hasn't realized he was missing but is very glad to see him. Without Amelia's sharp ears, the lamb's cries might have gone unheard in the traffic noise. Melissa calls it "the lamb Amelia saved."

It doesn't take long for Amelia's natural independence to appear. She's fearless. If Melissa's energy is flagging midafternoon when it's time to once again check on the flock, Amelia puts down her knitting, an activity I just do *not* understand, and leaps up from her chair. "I'll do it." She kicks the four-wheeler into first gear and cautiously putters toward the nearest gate. Amelia can recognize if a ewe is in labor and will radio back for Melissa.

Melissa and Amelia fall back into the rhythms established the first year, but their teamwork bumps up to a new level. Melissa knows the sorts of things that upset me, so a common refrain to Amelia becomes, "Don't tell Cath, but we're going to change this gate" or "Don't tell Cath, but we're going to put the sheep into the Creek Pasture." Later I ask Amelia what they've done that morning, and never understand why the poor thing hems and haws, unsure which activities have been on the "Don't tell Cath" list.

Melissa read that the placentas might attract predators, so to keep our sheep as safe as possible, she carries two long sticks and a paper bag on the four-wheeler. After all the day's crises have been resolved, and all the new lambs welcomed, Melissa and Amelia each take a stick and walk in a grid, searching for placentas. In my mind, doing such a job without complaint moves Amelia from Pasture Assistant to Pasture Goddess.

Amelia's a great sport. When Melissa discovers that those skinny gophers are once again digging an extensive subway system underneath our vineyard, she loads up her pellet gun. "Don't tell Cath, but we're going to shoot those SOBs."

For many of the hours I think those two are working in the pasture with sheep, they are really in the vineyard sprawled on the grass eating Oreos watching for gophers. It's a futile vigil, of course, but when the sun warms your skin, your belly is full of cookies, and you have the chance to fire a pellet gun, who cares?

One of Melissa's typical requests, made in all earnestness, is to ask other people to pretend to be sheep. She once practiced her sheep-shearing technique on me, minus the actual clippers. Another day she made me drop down onto all fours so she could figure out the straps on a harness for one of the rams.

Poor Amelia isn't immune. When they move the flock from the Tree Pasture to another run, the same place Amelia had found the lamb all alone, some lambs lag behind. Lambs don't understand gates, so if they don't follow right on the ewes' heels, they miss the gate.

Melissa and Amelia try herding the lambs toward the gate, but they all scatter in panic. "Moving lambs is like a fire drill in kindergarten," Melissa likes to say. We can often entice a ewe to come back and lead the lambs through the gate, but this time the ewes are too busy gobbling fresh grass to care about Melissa's problems. The lambs are all old enough that the moms aren't worried about keeping track of them every single minute.

"I need you to pretend to be a sheep," Melissa tells Amelia.

"You're kidding."

"Not at all. You're wearing a white T-shirt. Get down on your hands and knees and sort of baa. It'll work."

"You want me to baa."

"Kind of low and quiet. I'll go round the lambs up again, and try to drive them toward you."

Amelia good-naturedly shakes her head, then drops to all fours and begins bleating, truly a Pasture Goddess. Melissa circles back around the frantic lambs and begins encouraging them to move in Amelia's direction. They do. They see something sort of sheep height and sheep colored, emitting a fairly realistic sheep sound. Bleating encouragingly, Amelia crawls through the grass toward the gate. The lambs follow. More crawling, more bleating and the lambs are through the gate. They see the flock in the distance and launch themselves toward safety and fresh milk.

Amelia comes to help every year she's in college. However, it takes her a few years to understand that we don't ask for help merely to give her something to do, but because we really *need* her. She finally realizes this when, right in the middle of lambing, she must return to the Twin Cities to coach a girls' soccer game. The next day Melissa calls her, and in her most plaintive voice, demands to know, "When are you coming *home?*"

I would never have made it this deep into the farm's middle if Amelia hadn't replaced me in the pasture. Over the years she appears and disappears and reappears on the farm numerous times. We weren't able to adopt her, of course, but I remain deeply grateful that she adopted us, the Farmer and the Worry Wart.

My Nursery

Chaos is a friend of mine.

—Bob Dylan

Although spinning and birthing babies aren't my skills, I'm great at dealing with bottle lambs in the spring. I love the need to shift my focus away from everything else in my life—writing, speaking, friends, family, volunteering, cleaning the house—and focus on one thing: keeping the babies in my nursery safe, healthy, and well fed. I don't know this at the time, of course, but in a few years there will come a spring without lambs, without babies in the barn that depend on me for survival. Only then will I realize that I need them as much as they need me.

After a few years of lambing, we think we have the whole pro-cess figured out, but then one day we stand in the pasture admiring our first set of triplets. Two are round and plump, and hop around like healthy lambs. When they stand up, they stretch luxuriously, a sign of good health. But the third triplet is skinny and a little hunched over. He doesn't hop or stretch. We wait until the lambs are looking the other way, then we drop low and creep closer. Melissa's reflexes are quicker than mine, so she grabs the back leg of the skinny lamb. Got him!

The lamb's belly isn't full and tight with milk as it should be, so we conclude that the mother doesn't have enough milk to feed three babies. We do some research and learn that when a ewe is grazing on grass without any grain supplement, even though she can feed all three lambs for a couple of weeks, she'll reach a point where she doesn't have enough milk and one lamb will start falling behind.

So we begin automatically bringing in the smallest of triplets a few days after its birth and feeding it ourselves. The lamb grows faster and is happier. These types of lambs are called bottle lambs or bonus lambs. My mom, raised on that sheep ranch in southeastern Montana, calls them bum lambs. That's because in huge range flocks with 1,500 sheep, a lamb's pretty much on his own. If his mom doesn't have enough milk to feed him, the only way he'll survive is by sneaking up to other ewes and "bumming" a little milk before they realize the wrong lamb's taking a drink. Sheep are very fussy about that.

So my spring lambing ritual involves empty pop bottles and a bag of powdered milk so fine that opening the bag sends powder floating through the air to eventually settle onto my kitchen counter and floor. Add a bit of water, say on the dogs' feet, and you have a nice slurry of milk on everything.

Very young lambs need to be fed four times a day because their tummies are too small to hold much. It takes a while for a lamb to catch on to the bottle—the nipple doesn't feel right in the mouth, so the lamb spits it out. My first year as a lamb nanny was hard because I was terrified that the babies were going to starve. I'd spend ten minutes trying to get a new bottle lamb to nurse and end up in tears because she wouldn't. I'd go out to the barn every hour, sit down on an overturned five-gallon bucket, and try again.

Experience has taught me that a small lamb, once it consumes plenty of colostrum, might go a day without eating. By then it's very hungry and will suck on the bottle in desperation. Suddenly the incandescent light bulb goes on: *Holy Cow! There's milk in here!*

As our ewes mature and give birth to more and more triplets, I grow proficient at dealing with bottle lambs. My skills progress to the point I can feed five babies at once—two bottles in each hand, and one between them. But when the lambs are about three weeks old, they begin pushing each other off the bottles and maneuvering for the best spot. Chaos ensues. I must feed them one at a time, so I pick up a lamb and drape it across my lap. The weather is warm, the sun streaks through the open barn door, chickens coo happily around me, and I have a baby on my lap with a fiercely wagging tail making happy, slurpy sounds as it drinks. There are worse ways to spend an hour.

I don't like keeping them in the barn all day, so I set up a temporary pen outside with a mix of shade and sun. Some of the lambs quickly become so tame that I take them for short walks with me. One year, three little lambs follow me all around the yard, single file. Mary had a little lamb, indeed.

The craziest year, however, is when we have sixteen bottle lambs, thanks to triplets and a few mothering mishaps on the pasture. Feeding sixteen becomes a major nightmare, so we buy a bucket designed to feed many lambs at once. It's a white, five-gallon bucket with ten black nipples around the top. Running from each nipple down into the bucket is a clear plastic tube. All the lambs have to do is suck up the milk, and they're good to go.

The bucket, unfortunately, has been designed by an idiot. The milk must come all the way up the tube to reach the nipple, which means the lamb sucks and sucks, getting nothing but air. Just as milk reaches the nipple, the hungry lamb gives up. I stand there and watch the milk slide back down the tube. Acck! Try again! I get the lamb latched back onto the nipple, she sucks, and just as the milk reaches the top of the bucket she gives up. We need a bucket with the nipples on the bottom so the lambs get milk immediately. We would have invested in this, or in one of the many other devices shepherds have invented to make feeding bottle lambs easier, but then I figure something out. Many people living in the country want sheep but don't want to make their own.

I put an ad in the paper every spring, and nearly every year I have more orders for bottle lambs than I can fill. Melissa brings a triplet in, I feed it for a few days until it reliably drinks from the bottle, then I call the person at the top of the list.

When the very first buyer came, I carried the two lambs to their car, all the while filling the buyers' heads with everything they needed to know to keep the lambs healthy. We talked and talked, and I couldn't figure out why they weren't leaving.

Oh. I was still holding the lambs. They're hard to give up. Now I've learned to pick up the lamb, kiss its little head, then hand it immediately to the new owner before I change my mind. I'm not embarrassed they see me kiss the lamb because I want them to know the lamb is valued, and that I expect them to value it as well. As each car drives away, I sigh, missing the lambs already.

A Gaggle
of Goddesses

It's the friends you can call up at 4:00 AM that
matter.

—MARLENE DIETRICH

Amelia helps us until she graduates from college. Then the next
May she gets a summer job crewing for a tall-masted charter sail-
boat off the coast of Maine and is unavailable to help. What?
She'd rather have a sailing adventure and earn money than spend
two more weeks outside in the rain and mud, surrounded by babies? What is *with* kids these days?

Of course, she's no longer a teenager but a confident young
woman who can't build her life around helping us every May.
Melissa and I look at each other. Going back to having me as her

full-time pasture assistant doesn't appeal to either of us. A few days every spring is bad enough—but the entire three weeks?

As the next lambing season nears, I put out the word for "Amelia substitutes" and our friend Mary H., the one who'd dubbed me Mrs. Muffin, steps up to the plate. Mary brings her sharp wit and great laugh. After a week with us, having been peed on and pooped on and stepped on—all by sheep—Mary is both exhausted and exhilarated. She finds the whole experience "mind-blowing." As a horse person, Mary wanted to use her knowledge of cutting horses out of a herd, but thanks to the flocking behavior of sheep, horse techniques won't work. Mary quickly comes to appreciate Melissa's ability to see the world through the eyes of a sheep, and she starts doing the same thing. Soon the two of them work well together, almost without speaking, finding the same rhythm that Melissa and Amelia share. Mary calls it a ballet, a sort of pas de deux between shepherd and sheep. I call it a damned relief that I don't have to be out there myself in Full Anxiety Mode.

When Mary arrives, I list the ground rules: Always close gates behind you. Never go into the ram pen by yourself. And no naming anything. The second day she's here, Mary comes in from the pasture bubbling over with the birth she's witnessed. "Brutus Maximus is so huge."

"No naming the animals," I remind her.

The next day, she tells me about Hoppy McHopper, who does much leaping straight up into the air.

"No naming the animals."

"Oh, yeah, right."

A few days later Melissa and Mary roar up on the four-wheeler with an impossibly small lamb in Mary's arms. They'd gone out early in the morning to check on the ewes. Through the fog, they saw a ewe on the crest of the East Pasture hill. One new lamb stood beside her, and two lay on the ground. The women's hearts sank. The ewe had triplets, but two were dead. They motored close enough to see the dead lambs were covered in blood, as if the ewe had never cleaned them off. But when the smallest of the "dead" lambs started to move, Melissa and Mary flung up their hands. "It's alive!" they screamed. Mary caught the lamb and quickly tucked it inside her jacket to warm it up. Melissa determined that the other lamb was, sadly, dead, then quickly examined the standing lamb. It had a nice belly so it had nursed. The tiny baby in Mary's arms had not.

They call ahead, so by the time they reach the house I've thawed some frozen colostrum. I cannot believe how small the lamb is, maybe three pounds instead of the usual six to ten pounds. Melissa threads the rubber tube down its throat and I pour in the warm colostrum. I set up a heating pad in a box and the lamb spends the day in the entryway. Now and then I let Sophie, our maternal half Great Dane, come inspect the lamb. I let her give the lamb a thorough licking because I think the stimulation will help.

Later that day Mary calls on the walkie-talkie. "How's Little Bit? Is he eating?"

Little Bit?

I give up. Little Bit sleeps in his box on the floor in Mary's room that first night, so they totally bond. The next day he's drinking enthusiastically and in a few hours he's climbing out of the box and peeing on the floor. Mary spends every spare minute cuddling the lamb she considers to be a real fighter. He'd been born during a cool night, had no nourishment, yet had survived.

A few days later he's out in the barn cavorting with babies over twice his size. I keep him longer than usual to make sure he's healthy, then I find a great home for him. Mary reluctantly hands the baby over to the young woman, glaring at me. I'm not sure she's ever forgiven me for selling Little Bit.

In the years since, Mary has come to realize it isn't a great idea to get too attached to any of the babies, so the naming has slowed down a bit. She just calls them all "Lambie Doodle."

Melissa has her pasture goddesses, but I am the Goddess of Laundry. One day after a ewe gives birth, Mary brings in a bag full of dirty towels that they'd used to clean off lambs. I gingerly carry the bag to the washing machine, avert my eyes, and add it to the load of jeans. All goes well. But when the washer's done and I'm pulling Melissa's jeans from the load of clean clothing, something cold and long and slimy leaps from the jeans and wraps itself around my wrist several times. I shriek, but only in a brave, mature way, then see this same filmy stuff on Melissa's clean pants, one glob right next to my other hand.

I summon Melissa and Mary to the laundry room. "What is this? What is this? What is this?" (An effective technique for communicating distress is to ask the same question several times in a loud, possibly frantic voice.)

Melissa pulls the goop off the pants with her bare hands, examines it, then pronounces it to be the film or sac that the lambs are born in, sort of a biological Saran Wrap. It must have been on one of the towels. I might have begun jumping up and down at this point.

Mary grins but shakes her head. "What's the big deal? At least it's clean." She's grown far too comfortable with sheep bodily fluids, which is why she is a Pasture Goddess.

Ugly rumors have begun circulating that I then walked around the laundry room shaking my hands and saying, "Icky, icky, icky." These rumors are totally unfounded.

Mary helps as long as she can but then must return to her life. Enter Bonnie, a high school English teacher who calls herself a farmaholic, just the sort of person we love. She's also the woman who'd been so disappointed during shearing when I'd decided she lacked the weight to stomp the wool. Once I get to know her better, I realize she has such determination and drive that she would have simply *imagined* herself heavier and done a fine job of packing those fleeces.

School's out late May, so she joins us for the last week of lambing after Mary has left. Bonnie settles quickly into our routine. She's fearless, not surprising considering her career choice. She drives the four-wheeler, chases sheep, gives shots, does everything. But there's one thing she only does twice, and then declines. Putting the ear tag into a lamb's ear requires punching through the thin skin. The lambs jerk because it hurts, and Bonnie decides she's going to lose her lunch if she does any more ear tags.

Having new people on the farm forces us to slow down and see the process through their eyes. Bonnie finds the whole experience of birth intense and moving. One day she's in the pasture by herself, keeping an eye on a ewe in labor while Melissa takes a break. After a long labor, the ewe, standing up, gives birth to twins. Bonnie watches, marveling that fifteen minutes after arriving into the world by landing on their heads, both lambs are on their feet and nursing. Many a time she and Melissa stand in the pasture watching a birth, and Bonnie wipes away tears, complaining about the wind in her eyes.

She, too, loves walking the pasture searching for placentas. This is clearly the test to use when weeding out potential pasture goddesses. Hand them a long stick stained on one end with old blood, and a paper bag, and ask them to pick up stringy placentas that may be very dry or alarmingly fresh.

I love these women, but I do worry about their sanity. However, they aren't alone. Rancher Pachy Burns, who raises 800 sheep out west, has women flocking to her ranch to help with lambing every year. Some even pay to come. I wonder if Amelia, Mary, and Bonnie would still come if we started charging them. Perhaps we could advertise online: "Come run around the pasture until you're winded beyond belief! Find yourself covered in pee, poop, and placenta! Experience the emotional ups and downs of farming! Only $99.95 per day."

I know that lambing has enriched the lives of our pasture goddesses, increased their confidence, and given them a perspective they might not find living in the city. Continuing to farm just to provide people with this rich experience doesn't make sense, but it does make it harder to stop. It feels as if we're part of a web, one of the slender but strong threads that help city dwellers retain a connection to a way of life that, for most people, disappeared decades ago.

A Cure for
Writer's Block

Writing is 90 percent procrastination: reading
magazines, eating cereal out of the box, watching infomercials. It's a matter of doing everything you can to avoid writing.

—Paul Rudnick

There's no escaping a farm. The farm comes into the house on our
boots and jackets, and on the feet of our dogs. On bad days, I want
to be gone. Yet I can hear the animals outside, and if someone's in
distress and Melissa's gone, I can't ignore the problem. These are
my animals, too, and I care deeply for them.

For me, there's no escaping the worry. I wonder if worrying
burns up calories. Worrying about newborn lambs is just the tip of
the iceberg for me, as there are so many other things that can go

wrong on the farm. I can lie awake all night imagining lambs stuck in badger holes, or lambs lost in the woods, or lambs being stalked by coyotes.

I worry about my relationship. Melissa and I are approaching thirty years together. Holy Frijoles. Not to get all hung up on symbolism, but my parents divorced after thirty years. I see my parents in so many aspects of myself that this causes some anxiety, and it isn't helped when I hear on NPR that more people in their fifties are getting divorced than ever before. How do these people decide that life would be better by making a huge change than by staying put and finding a way to make things better? Is the situation too horrible to bear? Or too routine? Does the mountain called Going It Alone look more easily scaled than the mountain of Making It Work?

A relationship is like a well-running car—you don't think to appreciate that it starts every day and gets you where you need to go. Only when it breaks down do you pay attention. I don't judge others for ending relationships—my parents both seem very happy with their new lives—but the closer I come to that thirty-year mark with Melissa, the more I wonder: How do people make it that far?

We rarely pay attention to middles. Perhaps we ignore them because they're problematic. The middles of our beds often sag. The middles of our bodies sag. The middle of a long story told by your brother-in-law is likely to sag, and so you'll need another beer to stay focused. Everyone needs a reason to keep going when they're in the middle.

The middle of a long-term relationship can't compete with the beginning. All around us, people—young, middle-aged, and elderly—are beginning new relationships, causing a buzz among family and friends. We're energized by beginnings because they remind us of our own. Middles can't compete with the ends, either. When I encounter a recently divorced friend, here's what pushes my curiosity button: What caused the breakup? How did this happen? I find myself trying to be supportive and discreet, but inside I'm really desperate for details. A fight over money? Infidelity? Boredom? Some other deal breaker I've never heard of before? Perhaps I will see something in the sad tale to help me avoid my own relationship "crash-and-burn."

The middle is full of cycles that can break a relationship at any time, which is why we should give ourselves more credit for getting this far. My first years together with Melissa were intense and amazing. Then we drifted into complacency, taking each other's love for granted. The igniting spark of our relationship faded into mortgages and dental bills and fights over spending money. We drifted apart, far enough that something—I can't even remember what—shocked us back into reconnecting. We worked harder at communicating. It was intense, and wonderful. Then we drifted back into complacency again until we once more shocked ourselves back into the relationship, and the cycle began anew. It's like showing up in the emergency room every few years and being zapped with paddles before it's too late.

I yearn for something, but I can't put my finger on it. Do I yearn to know if—by following Melissa onto this farm—I've wasted the middle of my life? Am I supposed to be doing something else? I feel like the kid at the piñata party who's been blindfolded, then spun around and around until he's too dizzy to confidently take a step forward. Life has spun me around and suddenly I'm unsure of my next step.

Something feels off. I should be happier than I am. I should be relaxed and content and comfortable in my own skin. Melissa's not at her usual best, either. She's tired all the time. She's spinning her wheels, working harder and harder and getting less done. She gets sad for no apparent reason, although her mom's declining health and odd behavior might have something to do with that. But even though we still laugh every day, the laughter's growing a bit weak. I long to hit the open road and leave our responsibilities behind. We'll take a few boxes of books, Melissa's fly-fishing rods, and our dogs, and we'll have all we need to be happy.

I research RVs online and discover the Jayco Melbourne, a snazzy little Class C home on wheels. We could sell the farm, buy the Melbourne, and have enough left over to stash away for a life-time of gas refills and KOA fees.

My escapist reverie is interrupted by my need to meet a pub-lishing deadline, so I file it away for later. I spend ten grueling days writing from 5:00 AM until 8:00 PM, trying to finish a draft of my current book. My brain is totally fried, but there's no time in my schedule to stop. I have to get back to work. Instead, I look out the dining room window and notice that something looks odd in the pasture. The sheep are closer than they should be, and there is *lots* of baa-ing. Melissa is asleep, trying to shake one of the head-aches that have plagued her for twenty-five years, so I slip on my purple Birkies and tramp out to investigate.

What a mess. Half the flock is where it should be, with water but nothing left to eat. The other half has broken through a fence into the next run up, where they have food but no water. Mamas and babies are separated by an electric fence and crying for each other. On top of that, two ewes have managed to find their way into a third paddock altogether.

I mentally rub my hands together in anticipation. Moving sheep is challenging and fun, and if you're lucky it might go well. Also, it's a great way to put off writing. I may lack confidence in my ability to create rich characters, but I understand a sheep's flight zones. I know how to lead them and how to drive them. I haven't been raising sheep all these years without paying attention. And because the flock is still inside the perimeter fence, all the sheep are safe, so I can relax and focus on solving the problem.

I find where they've broken through the fence, so I disconnect the electricity and begin trying to get the two main groups together. I manage to get both groups walking alongside each other, separated by the three-wire fence, until we reach an opening at the end of the fence where the two groups merge. Mamas and babies run for each other. I lock everyone into the new paddock and bring them a water trough, which the thirsty animals nearly swamp as they push each other aside to drink.

Then I work on the two ewes stuck in the third spot, all three of us running back and forth, back and forth, until I'm hot and sweaty and the ewes are most unhappy, but I finally get them into the right place. Moving an entire flock is easier than moving two sheep.

As I'm walking back to the house, Melissa shows up on the four-wheeler. I'm proud to explain everyone is once again in the right place. Melissa is surprised I didn't wait for her. I'm surprised, too, but then it hits me. Chasing sheep, even though it's 90°F out, was exactly what I'd needed. The activity uses different muscles, both body and brain, and gives me instant feedback and satisfaction. I don't worry about the farm or about my relationship or about where I'm supposed to be in life. I just do what needs to be done, and it feels good.

I climb back up to the house, change out of my sweaty clothes, eat two banana Popsicles, then start writing again.

Enough
Happy Endings?

Weave me a rope that will pull me through
these impossible times.

—TIM FINN

On a farm, death is such a regular visitor that I'm no longer surprised when he drops by. We might lose a sheep to a disease. A
chicken might be taken by a hawk. We're going to lose a sheep to
old age, for No. 66 is slowing down. How long will she live?

When we started farming and animals died, I thought we were
terrible farmers. But other farmers reassured me, shaking their
heads and repeating the common refrain: "Where there's livestock, there's dead stock." It's one I now share with new farmers so
they know what's coming.

The Pasture Goddesses—Amelia, Mary, and Bonnie—are incredibly brave women, staying by Melissa's side even when things get hard. Over 1,300 lambs have been born on this farm, and of those, we've lost only fifty that were either stillborn or died soon after birth. We feel pretty good about that. Why is it, though, that even when the pasture pulses with life, the losses and tragedies loom so large in memory?

One of the first years Amelia helped us, she and Melissa found a ewe who'd given birth to triplets but a week later was very ill. Melissa wondered if there might be a problem inside. A terrible thought occurred. What if the ewe had gestated quadruplets? Amelia and Melissa caught the ewe and Melissa found another lamb inside. It was, of course, dead, and had begun to decay. They called the vet, and he determined that the ewe was beyond saving. This wasn't anyone's fault, for the ewe had given no indication she hadn't finished lambing. Yet this sad event tripled Melissa's vigilance on the pasture, and she often checks to make sure every single lamb is out. We've never had a repeat problem.

One morning Melissa called me on the walkie-talkie. So much was going wrong that she needed another pair of hands. In addition to lots of newborns that needed welcoming, there was a tragedy. Somehow a ewe had, midlabor, laid down on the flexible three-wire electric fence. The fence pulses on and off, and though it's not strong enough to kill a full-grown sheep or human, it's not as kind to lambs. Two lambs had been born directly onto the wires trapped under the ewe, and both were dead.

I hesitate even to write these stories because they're so hard, but it's part of what farmers sign up for when they devote their life to caring for animals. Bad things happen. Not often, but still, death comes more regularly than for most nonfarmers. Melissa processes death by talking about it, telling the story over and over to any friend or family member who happens to call or stop by. Eventually she works through her pain and can move on. I deal with it by *not* talking about it with anyone, by *not* listening to Melissa tell the stories. When I can stand to be in the room when Melissa shares a hard story, then I know I'm moving through the loss.

Complaining about death when it's part of your job seems silly, especially since what we've experienced is *nothing* compared to real disasters. The barn of a local sheep dairy burned to the ground, killing hundreds of sheep. Turkey barns are destroyed in storms, killing thousands of turkeys. Floods drown livestock that farmers or ranchers are unable to rescue. During disease scares like "mad cow" in the United Kingdom, millions of healthy animals were killed in hopes the disease wouldn't spread. A local elk herd, nearly 700 tawny beasts with towering antlers, was "eliminated" because one of them was found to have chronic wasting disease. *This* is a disaster. The owner, a California investment company, couldn't feel any emotional loss and was compensated financially, but someone had cared for those elk, and to those people, having sharpshooters kill all those animals had to be devastating.

Falling into the "disaster" category was the fire on my grand-mother's ranch forty years ago. My grandfather had died of a heart attack before I was born, but my Montana grandmother continued to raise sheep. I wish I'd known sheep were going to be in my life because I would have asked so many questions. Unfortunately, she died before I'd even met Melissa.

When I was about thirteen, my mom and sister and I were vis-iting the ranch in July. The dry land was 2,000 acres of tinder waiting for a match. One evening a bolt of lightning streaked down and became that match.

A neighbor called, reporting a thread of smoke rising from Grandma's land. Other neighbors roared up in pickups. They loaded the vehicles with barrels of water and burlap bags. My aunt stayed behind to watch us children, and my mom hopped in the pickup with Grandma and spun out into the dark.

At one point my aunt was worried about everyone, so we drove down the road until she could see Mom and Grandma in the distance, fighting the fire. We stood there in our cotton nightgowns, watching the flames dance across the range, black smoke billowing darker than the sky. Time has now created in my memory a conflagration as dramatic as the burning of Atlanta in *Gone with the Wind*.

The next morning I woke up to find my mom and grandma sitting in the kitchen, cupping coffee mugs in their hands, shoulders slumped as if their bones had melted in the fire. "Did the sheep survive?" I asked.

"Let's go look," Grandma replied, but the answer was already in her voice.

Mom and I rode in the cab of the pickup with Grandma, her rifle mounted on the back window. Now and then we'd find a group of live sheep, huddled together. Grandma made note of where they were so she could come back later and round them up. More often, however, we stopped at group after group of dead sheep that had been trapped by a bluff. Now and then Grandma would bend over a sheep that was still alive but too far gone to save, shake her head, and climb back into the truck.

Grandma would not shoot the animals in front of her city granddaughter, so after she returned us to the ranch house, she went back and shot each animal that needed dispatching. I understand why she did that alone. It must have been unbearably hard.

Our pasture goddesses keep returning every spring, so we must be doing something right. I remind myself that death isn't as constant as it seems. Many times, I hear a ewe cry, so I head for the pasture. The ewe's lamb might be asleep, sick, or dead. I walk the pasture until I spy a spot of white. As I approach, I can see the tiny chest lifting with each inhalation. The lamb is alive, but so deep into her own "lambie doodle" dream that she didn't hear her mother. Few actions are as satisfying as gently picking up a sleeping lamb, tucking it against your chest so it can feel your heartbeat, then rejoining the flock and placing the lamb right in front of its frantic mother.

There are more than enough happy endings on this farm.

Does This Bale
Make Me Look Fat?

Stressed spelled backwards is desserts. Coinci-
dence? I think not!

—AUTHOR UNKNOWN

Every fall, Melissa prepares for winter by using the tractor to set
out big round bales, which are about 1,400 pounds each, and five
feet tall by five feet wide. The sheep will eat on the bales all winter, since in Minnesota grass doesn't thrive in minus 30°F temper-
atures, buried under four feet of snow. We enclose each large bale
with slotted panels to keep the sheep from wasting hay. Their
heads fit comfortably through the slots so they can eat the hay
without climbing all over the bales.

One year, we decide to save ourselves some time so we move
four bales together, then put panels around this quartet. Imagine

four gigantic Tootsie Rolls stacked on their ends, side by side. We'll save time because the sheep will have to eat four entire bales before we must move the panels to the next set of four.

Unfortunately, our clever idea turns out to be not so clever. It doesn't take long for the sheep to somehow defeat our panel system, and soon they're frolicking on *top* of the four bales. Not surprisingly, one slips, and her back end wedges itself in the convergence of the four bales. Melissa tries for half an hour to free her, pushing, shoving, and murmuring words of comfort and encouragement. Finally she appears in my office. "I need your help."

I change into my work clothes, a bit peeved at the interruption. I am, after all, my ornery grandmother's granddaughter. I march out to the hay bales, letting the gate slam behind me, then confront the ewe, who's basically a ballerina on tiptoes wearing a tutu of hay bales. "Hey!" I yell.

The ewe shoots straight up into the air, slides down the bale, and runs off. Melissa's mouth drops open. "Wow," she says.

"Anytime," I reply, pleased no middle fingers were required. Then I return to the house, change out of my work clothes and start writing again.

An hour later Melissa is back. "Got another one." I go through the clothes-changing routine, slam the gate, and confront the ewe in the same situation as the last one, her backside jammed down between the bales. "Hey!" I say.

Nothing happens. She stares at us. This one is obviously stuck, and good. We slide a long two-by-four in between the bales, trying to push her butt up. The two-by-four snaps. While Melissa returns to the barn, I hang out with the ewe, who by now is eating from the bales forming her prison. I'm about to remind her that eating isn't going to help the situation, but since I tend to eat more when

stressed as well, I skip the lecture. As she munches, I begin fanta-
sizing about a slice of bread, slathered with butter. Or a toasted
bagel, slathered with butter.

Melissa brings out a long metal pole, which we poke between
the bales. The sheep squirms at this, perhaps not liking the feel of
a metal pole being poked at her butt, but she remains firmly
lodged. We can't use the tractor to move the bales because there's
a fence in the way.

By now it's dusk, and it's getting hard to see. Melissa brings
down the pickup, a chain, and a grappling hook. She sinks the
hook into the top of the bale, the only part she can reach, drives
away, and the hook comes sliding out. We repeat this step an embarrassing number of times, succeeding only in moving one bale
about two feet. The ewe drops down onto her hooves but now is
totally surrounded by the bales. I'm getting discouraged. "Maybe
we should bring her a bucket of water and deal with it tomorrow."

Finally Melissa bravely takes the hook in hand, and literally
dives up and over where two bales meet. Her head is down in the
ewe's little prison. All I can see are her boots up in the air. "I'm
stuck," she says.

"Maybe I should bring you a bucket of water and—"

"Not funny. Stuck tight—can't breathe—hook's in bottom of
bale—pull with truck."

I'm terrified the hook will slide out and impale Melissa. But after a bit of arguing on my part and some gasping on Melissa's, I
jump into the pickup and drive forward until I hear a shout. I leap
out in time to see Melissa slide to the ground, and the ewe spring
over her through the opening I've made.

The ewe bleats all the way up to the barn, no doubt composing
her complaint to the Society for the Prevention of Cruelty to An-

imals. Melissa and I return to the house, relieved to have solved the problem. No fences were broken. No damage was done to the pickup. No buildings were dented. The sheep is safe. And no one—human or ovine—was impaled by the bale hook or crushed by a hay bale. These moments in my life are oddly satisfying.

To celebrate, I consume both a slice of bread *and* a toasted bagel, both slathered in butter.

Tending the Vineyard

Grapes are the most noble and challenging of fruits.

—Malcolm Dunn, head gardener to
the Seventh Viscount Powerscourt, c. 1867

We keep our house stocked in wine by growing wine grapes. We don't make wine ourselves—that's a little too DIY for me—but sell the grapes to a winery. We carry buckets of grapes into the back door of the winery and walk out the front with many bottles of wine. It's a beautiful system.

When planted correctly (not upside down) it takes a grapevine about four years to mature and produce a crop. For each year leading to that fourth year, we pinch off the buds so the plants focus on making roots and growing stronger. Finally, Year Four arrives. We let the buds blossom into clusters of little fuzzy white things, which turn into grapes. Green for most of the summer, the grapes begin darkening in August. Plump, deep-red clusters hang heavy on the vines. In late August, Melissa and I attend the Minnesota State Fair to answer questions about growing grapes at the Grape Growers booth. We return home to find birds have consumed our entire crop.

One acre of grapes gone in about twelve hours. Nuts.

Every year after that, the battle against the birds starts in early August. One afternoon I see a flock of grackles rise up slowly from the vineyard. I imagine they are so stuffed with grapes they can barely fly. Furious, I retrieve our shotgun and load it as Melissa has taught me. I storm out to the middle of the vineyard, aim toward the sky and pull the trigger.

I'm not sure if I really ended up flat on my ass or if it just felt like it. My ears rang and my shoulder ached. I put the shotgun down, trembling. What was I thinking? There's no better way to understand the terrible power of a gun than to actually fire one.

The next summer when the birds return, I leave the shotgun locked in the gun cabinet. Melissa's gone for the day and the birds have begun swarming all over the grapes. I must do something, so I grab a massive stick, a book, a chair, and a cell phone; then I spend the warm, sunny afternoon in the vineyard. I read for a while, then walk one row of the 400-foot vineyard, banging on the trellis posts. The vibrating trellis wires send the birds flying. I return down another row, call a friend to complain of the rigors of farming, then settle in to read a few more chapters. It's a ludicrous and futile activity, of course, but I must have needed an afternoon of reading and banging on posts.

Shotguns and banging posts aren't realistic, long-term solutions. Melissa read that Tina Turner music had been effective in keeping birds away at airports, so she runs speaker wires from the shed to the vineyard and begins serenading the birds (and the neighbors) with "Proud Mary" and "What's Love Got to Do with It." Turns out the birds in this area are hard-core Tina fans and tell all their friends.

Desperate now, the next year we purchase expensive mesh netting and begin covering the vineyard every August, just as the grapes are reaching Nummy Stage. Every few days one of us walks the vineyard and frees any birds that have worked their way into the nets but can't get back out.

Grapevines require lots of pruning, which means holding one's arms up high for long periods of time. Melissa has been prone to headaches for most of her adult life, so pruning becomes a most painful chore. Between my paying job teaching writing and working on my own writing, I don't have much time for the vineyard. Melissa does her best, but without regular pruning, a vineyard becomes a teenager with bed head.

My vineyard job is to mow the grass between the rows. The grass keeps down weeds and holds the soil in place on the gradual slope. I plug my MP3 player into my headphones, fill the old riding lawn mower with gas, and lose myself in the sun and music and grass-cutting satisfaction.

When the hour's over, returning to the shed requires that I drive down the sloping windbreak toward the barn, which is surrounded by cattle panel fencing, a heavy steel mesh with little give. One day everything on the mower fails at once. The brakes don't work. The engine's stuck in gear even as I shift from Drive to Neutral to Reverse to God-Help-Me-I'm-Going-to-Crash. I even turn off the ignition as I pick up speed. Nothing. I'm heading straight for the fence at the bottom of the hill.

Farming is a dangerous business. Tractors overturn. Implements maim. I knew it would happen to me one day. I just didn't think the moment would make me look so silly: bouncing down the hill on a little orange mower, clinging to the petite steering wheel, my mouth wide open to better let my scream escape. At the last minute I manage to turn the non-power-steering wheel to the right and bounce my way alongside the fence and down yet another hill. The mower finally comes to a halt in front of the barn. I slump over the sweaty steering wheel, exhausted after my brush with death.

We purchase a new mower.

Melissa cares deeply for the vineyard, even though she isn't able to give it the regular haircuts it needs. But she is able to spray the plants every ten days for mildew. Her options are to tote a backpack sprayer or drag a canister on a little dolly. Both lead to headaches, so she buys a small metal cart to pull behind the four-wheeler and tricks it out for vineyard duty, with tanks and a vertical boom to spray the vines at three different heights for complete coverage. Melissa is the most thorough person I know. No leaf shall go unsprayed.

Spraying works best without wind, and it doesn't stop blowing until dark, so Melissa begins her spraying job at 10:00 PM. During the summer I fall asleep to the soft putter of the four-wheeler as Melissa sprays one side of the row, then the other, row after row, her single headlight carving a narrow path through the warm darkness.

And here's a perfect example of how farming can be romanticized, even by the farmer herself. I'm lulled to sleep by the comforting image of Melissa happily spraying her vines. In reality, her four-wheeler headlight attracts every moth within miles. While I sleep, she's fighting off the moths flying in her face and crawling on her neck.

I like my version better.

The Perfect Nest

Young cat, if you keep your eyes open enough,
oh, the stuff you would learn! The most wonderful stuff!

—Dr. Seuss

After years of draining my writing energy, the farm slowly begins
to give back, with *Hit by a Farm*, and then *The Compassionate Carnivore*, a mix of memoir, nonfiction, and self-help. Yet the farm
continued to withhold ideas for children's stories. Farms should be
ripe with children's story ideas because farms play such a role in
their learning. Stephen Kellert, who studies animals and human
behavior, found that more than 90 percent of the characters used
to teach language and counting to young children are animals.

Yet I manage to go years without any decent ideas. But then
the Farm Story Goddess looks down upon our meager fifty acres,

where I sit dejectedly without inspiration, and graciously awards me two events that will generate a story.

The first event is the day in the barn when I hear something banging back in the corner behind a feed barrel. I timidly peer down into the darkness, afraid to see a rat. Instead, I see what looks like a chicken's body and a duck's head. Whoa. Gotta lay off the caffeine. I ignore my hallucination and continue with chores.

The next morning I hear the same banging, only this time when I look, I see what appears to be a duck's body with a chicken's head. Now I am worried, so I track down Melissa, who's out in the pasture fixing a fence. She knows exactly what I'm talking about. "A duck and chicken both laid an egg back there and neither wants to give up the nest." Later I find five hens in a nest box meant for one, basically stacked on top one another, each determined to lay her egg in that nest.

The second event is of a feline nature. We don't encourage stray cats to live in our barns or pastures because kittens can carry a disease that causes abortions in sheep. Not good. But when a half-grown orange-and-white cat shows up, so friendly he must have been dumped (by one of those irresponsible pet owners who should be abandoned in the middle of the Arctic Circle as punishment for doing this to a domestic pet), we fall in love and name him Oliver. He takes up residence in the hay mow, the warmest, driest, safest place on the farm.

The next year, Oliver himself adopts a half-grown cat, but the only thing we ever see of this guy is the flash of his orange tail as he runs from us. All winter long we feed two cats, one of which is terrified of us. But then Melissa begins leaving a saucer of milk in the barn. Within a few days the orange cat comes down the wooden ladder, sniffs the milk on Melissa's hands, and rolls over on his back as if to say he'll do anything for some milk.

Two cats—Oliver and Pumpkin—and many baby chicks and ducklings hatching every year would seem to be a bad combination. But Melissa scolds the cats whenever they look at the babies, and soon the boys figure out that if they're going to be allowed to stay, baby poultry are off limits. When Mama Duck has a batch of eighteen ducklings, she marches them past Oliver, stretched out on the barn floor. He watches, but he doesn't dare touch.

I begin to think—what if I write a story about a cat that wants to eat the eggs in a nest but instead ends up taking care of the babies that hatch from those eggs? And maybe there would be poultry that fight over the same nest. The result is *The Perfect Nest*.

For me, waiting for a picture book to make its way from a few scribbled notes in my notebook, to a typed manuscript given to the illustrator, to a series of sketches, to many finished paintings feels like a century, but when illustrator John Manders is finished, the story becomes a real book.

Here's the publisher's description: "Jack the cat is building the perfect nest. It's bound to attract the perfect chicken, who will lay the perfect egg, which will make the perfect omelet. And sure enough, a chicken shows up ('¡Caramba!') but so do a duck ('Sacré bleu!') and a goose ('Great balls of fire!'). Feathers get ruffled—and Jack gets much more than breakfast—in a funny tale rich in details with a sweet final twist."

After the book is published, I begin hearing fun stories from teachers who read the book to their class, then the next day all the first-graders run around the classroom exclaiming, "¡Caramba! Sacré bleu! Great balls of fire!"

Our dear Oliver died a few years later, and we were heartbroken. We adopted little Maisie and Eddie Velvet. Unfortunately,

Eddie was a roamer, and after we'd totally fallen for him, one day a year later he never returned home. Pumpkin and Maisie remain, and Maisie has learned the same lesson about baby poultry as Oliver and Pumpkin did. Paws *off*. She knows sparrows and mice are fair game, however, so she stalks them daily.

Because she loves us, and is a good provider, Maisie often shares her kill, leaving the only part of the mouse she doesn't eat on our front step. I've yet to come up with an idea for a children's book about these green, kidney-bean-sized large intestines, but perhaps one day my muse will return.

The Farmer's Wife

I love being married. It's so great to find that
special person you want to annoy for the rest
of your life.

—Rita Rudner

Women have farmed for millennia. Social scientists believe that
when humans first made the transition from hunting and gathering to agriculture, it was women who discovered how to domesti-
cate and cultivate plants. Women have farmed alongside men for
centuries on all continents and, in many countries, they still do.
It was not until the industrialization of agriculture that women
were shifted from being farmers to being farmers' wives.

According to the USDA Census of Agriculture, women are rediscovering their roots. Women farmers increased by 30 percent
between 2002 and 2007, so now more than one in every ten U.S.
farms is run by a woman. This is great. Unfortunately, on those

farms "run" by men, many are actually run by both spouses, yet the man is the farmer, and the woman is the farmer's wife.

I've never aspired to be either a farmer or a wife; basically since I was nineteen, I never expected to be able to legally marry the person I loved. Although I call myself a farmer, Melissa is definitely the primary farmer and I'm the backup farmer. As for me fitting the old-fashioned stereotype of the "farmer's wife," well, not really. I don't can fruit and vegetables or make quilts, and I can't stand to weed, which is sort of a requirement if you're going to garden. I can make a mean batch of strawberry-rhubarb freezer jam, but that's about it. I'm happy to hang out laundry, as long as it's not too cold or windy.

A gazillion years after my realization at nineteen that I would never marry, the world has changed. It's now possible for me to not only be a farmer, but to also be a farmer's wife.

There isn't a deeply romantic moment when one of us kneels before the other and whips out a diamond ring. After this many years together, surprises are rare. In fact, when California legalizes marriage for everyone, and I look at her and say, "What do you think?" Melissa's response is something like a shrug, and "I don't think we need to do that." Perhaps we should have been more creative, like the guy in Yorkshire who proposed to his girlfriend by spelling out "Will you marry me?" in sheep. Of course, he first "wrote" the question in corn on the ground, then let his sheep eat the corn.

Three months later Melissa turns to me and says, "Yes."

"Yes, what?"

"Yes, I'd like to get married."

When I tell my straight friends I'm getting married, most are so happy they choke up. When I tell my gay friends, some are wildly happy for me, but I can tell others wonder what my choice means for their lives. And when I tell my parents and sister, I once again drag them into uncharted territory. Why enter into a marriage that will only be legal in a handful of states? How does one celebrate this event? What traditions of the legal-in-all-fifty-states marriage are appropriate and which should be rejected?

Melissa and I will fly to California. San Francisco City Hall will take care of the ceremony, but beyond that, what do I want? One tradition of marriage I reject immediately is the bridal registry. But my stepsister keeps at me until I cave and register at www.macys .com. The Web site recommends I choose 150 items for the celebration party we've planned, yet I'm appalled at the prices and feel weird picking out my own gifts. I choose seventeen items and stop. Since I'm not telling anyone I've registered, seventeen should be plenty.

Although I don't want a fancy white dress and veil, I do want flowers in my hands. I call a charming San Francisco florist and order six bouquets of white lilies for me, Melissa, and the four California friends who'll be with us.

The night before we leave for San Francisco, I talk with a friend about marriage. We agree it's silly when people expect to feel differently about a relationship because a judge says some words. Melissa and I have made it this long without a marriage license, thank you very much. Getting married won't change anything.

But when Melissa and I step into the San Francisco City Hall, with its grand marble staircase and soaring ceilings, something happens. I realize for the first time the significance of what I'm about to do. I'm going to publicly declare my love and commitment to another person. We are legally joining our lives together. A man and woman are being married in the rotunda at the top of the grand staircase, which chokes me up. Twenty minutes later two men exchange vows, and I get another lump in my throat. After another couple marries, I take Melissa aside. "I think I'm going to cry during our ceremony."

"Oh, yeah," she says, patting my hand.

Turns out we both do, but we also manage to squeak out "I do" when asked. And then we are done. We are married. I feel light and insanely happy all that day. In fact, for our entire stay in California, I feel light and insanely happy. I wonder about the source of this feeling—security? recognition? affirmation?—but I know full well that when we return to our farm in Minnesota, this amazing, giddy feeling will fade. But it doesn't. Melissa feels it, too. For some people, marriage *does* change how you feel. Suddenly I'm angry at the world for denying me this feeling for so many years.

A package shows up on our doorstep, a gift chosen from my macys.com registry. Cool. Perhaps I'd been too hasty in damning the registry idea. I could get used to gifts spontaneously appearing. In fact, I wonder if I can combine the state-by-state extension of marriage rights with the whole bridal registry thing. Each time a state legalizes my marriage, it will be like getting married again. I'll send out e-mail notices: "We're now legal in Alabama. Hurrah! We're registered at macys.com." The stream of gifts should last for years.

But then the people of California pass Proposition 8 and my marriage to Melissa enters the Twilight Zone. Eventually the California Supreme Court decides that Proposition 8 will stand, but so, too, will the legality of the 18,000 marriages that took place before it passed.

What a relief. Now I won't have to give the wedding gifts back.

We settle into married life, which is, of course, no different than our life before we stood in the marble rotunda and recited our vows. But we do feel different. Perhaps that's why I've decided that it's not only okay to be a farmer, but it's also okay to be a farmer's wife.

Just Ducky

I hope you love birds too. It is economical. It
saves going to heaven.

—EMILY DICKINSON

Although our farm may be built around sheep, other animals always seem to work their way into our lives. The llamas have a job to do, so they support themselves. The beef steers are here to be raised as meat, so they make sense, and the chickens lay eggs, so they're an obvious choice as well.

But the peacocks? The little golden pheasants? The ducks? Melissa has always had a weakness for birds. We got rid of our two peacocks because they were defecating on my car. Melissa missed them so much she built a thirty-by-twenty-foot pen with room for them to fly up on perches, and the peacocks were back. They did a little too much breeding, however, and soon the pen was full.

Melissa eventually found the peacocks new homes. The old guy, Ben, remains, as do the pheasants to keep him company.

The golden pheasants are sweet, and they make soft chittering sounds when you enter the pen. Pharoah is yellow and blue and green and ruby—a dramatic splash of color in the grass. Trixie is the female, a demure mottled brown. Life is about to get very confusing for both, however, as after her most recent molt, Trixie's feathers are growing back as if she were a male. She's beautiful, but still, it's a little freaky.

Ducks aren't on our farm for profit. They're here because Melissa adores them, and because baby ducklings are funny little peeping balls that enliven the barnyard. The comings and goings of ducks from this farm, both planned and unplanned, illustrate the revolving door that operates, on a much larger scale, for a farm's livestock. We've had many more sheep and goats than anyone wants to track without a computer program, but the duck numbers are a little more manageable.

Although some years, it doesn't feel that way. Mama Duck and Mr. Duck make batch after batch of babies, and Mama Duck keeps every single one of them safe with her fierce posture and angry hissing. Both techniques convince me to keep my distance, as does the memory of her incredibly strong bill clamped onto my knee.

Then one day Mama Duck disappears. Just gone. She wouldn't have wandered far from the barn, so something took her. Melissa is stunned. Even I miss Mama Duck.

Melissa keeps one of her offspring and names her Daphne. Daphne and Mr. Duck have many ducklings over the years. Melissa sells most of the ducks to Harry's Chicken Ranch. Harry is sort of a poultry broker. But one fall when the elderly man becomes ill and stops dealing poultry for a while, the current batch of duck-lings grows into adults. Soon most are nearly as large as Mr. Duck himself.

This bunch is rowdy. They begin going on long-distance walks, terrorizing the neighborhood. We start getting calls. "I just passed a bunch of ducks walking down the road. Might be yours," says one neighbor. I walk down the long driveway and herd them home.

"There are some ducks in our lawn," says another neighbor far-ther down the road. "They might be yours." Melissa drives down there, but by now the ducks are all strong flyers, so they take off for home. Then a third neighbor calls, reporting the ducks are on her driveway, the farthest they've traveled. "They might be yours," she says.

I'm walking to the mailbox anyway, so I just keep going and find the ducks. I say, "Hey, you're not supposed to be here." The ducks perform their awkward running takeoff and soar over my head.

All except one. He either hasn't figured it out or is just too tired to get his carcass off the ground. I can relate. Still, I can't just leave the guy to find his way home alone, so I escort him back. Even a duck in a big hurry moves slowly, so what should be a ten-minute walk home becomes thirty-five. We have a nice chat, though, so the time passes pleasantly. As we stroll, I decide there is nothing so endearing as the backside of a Muscovy duck pa-tiently waddling homeward.

Melissa keeps three females from another batch and names them Veronica, Chloe, and Helen. She still has Ping II, the duck she raised by hand. Sadly, eventually Daphne disappears. There are many benefits to free-range poultry, but safety from predators isn't one of them.

Then one day I find Molly, our hunting dog, chewing on Ping in the backyard. The duck wandered into the Dog Zone and Molly killed him.

The next year, we sell Chloe to Harry because we're sick of her attitude. She sits on the nest just fine, hatches her eggs, but then is either unwilling, or unable, to keep track of her babies. Many of them disappear.

At least we still have Veronica and Helen. Then a predator, probably a weasel, kills Veronica near the driveway but finds her too heavy to carry away. Mr. Duck, now quite elderly, falls ill and dies.

We're down to Helen, a white duck with black wing tips. Melissa worries she's lonely, but in inimitable duck fashion, Helen stays busy eating grasshoppers and earthworms out of Melissa's hand, patrolling the barnyard, and taking noisy baths every day.

Naming the peacocks and the golden pheasants and the ducks (and the llamas and the rams and the roosters) soon proves too much for even me, and my principles collapse under the weight of all those names. We continue to sell all our bottle lambs, but one year we keep two for ourselves: an all-black lamb and an all-white one. We're fascinated by the all-black girl, and Melissa likes the genetics of the all-white girl's mother.

I feed them four times a day, then three, then they're old enough to live with the flock and add grass to their diet. The two of them hang out together because it takes them a while to really connect with the other sheep. To feed them, I walk out to the pasture and call "Hey, lambies." In this context "lambies" isn't really a name, but just a generic noun. Please note the use of the lower case. Anyway, after I shout this noun-that-isn't-a-name, out from the flock shoot two little rockets, butts dropped low to increase their speed, each on fire to be the first to the bottle.

The problem is that I keep forgetting the ear tag numbers of the two lambs. I return to the house and report that the black girl has drunk the whole bottle, but the white girl hasn't. It doesn't take long before "the black girl" becomes Black Girl, and "the white girl" becomes White Girl.

Oops. I have named two of our ewes. That's just ducky. Really. What an idiot. I can't believe I've done this. And they aren't even interesting names.

We don't go down without a fight. Melissa gives each lamb her adult ear tag: The black lamb will be Orange 1. The white lamb will be Orange 3. "We'll use these numbers," she says.

For a few days we do our best. "Orange 3 nearly pulled the bottle from my hand this afternoon." "I think Orange 1's fleece is getting lighter from the sun."

But it's too late. We slide back into White Girl and Black Girl without a word. Perhaps we aren't the tough, bad-ass farmers we think we are.

The Incredible
Shrinking Jeans

If I had been around when Rubens was painting, I would have been revered as a fabulous
model. Kate Moss? She would have been the
paintbrush.

—DAWN FRENCH

Through some sort of weird sunspot activity, or terrorist plot, or
government secret ray gun, my jeans are getting smaller. I must
buy another pair. But after I eat less, drink less wine, and actually
get off my butt thirty minutes a day, the old jeans once again expand to fit me. It's a puzzling thing.

And it doesn't just happen once. It happens every few years.
Luckily, the universe always manages to expand my shrunken
jeans so I can wear them again.

Until now. The magic is gone. I must not only buy a larger pair of jeans, but then these shrink as well. I eat less. I drink less wine. I move more. And still, nothing changes. My mother has warned me that one day my jeans will shrink and stay shrunk, but I don't believe her. I'm a baby boomer. What happened to the bodies of my mom's generation will not happen to mine. It's unthinkable.

Shrinking pants are more than just an inconvenience. They interfere with farming. One early fall day I flee the farm for a meeting, wearing my favorite turquoise top and my favorite pair of jeans, which have shrunk just enough that I look good, but with enough "give" that I can actually drive sitting down.

When I arrive home, Melissa is out in the pasture moving the sheep. It seems to be taking longer than it should, so I slip on my barn Birkies to help. No reason to change into my roomy bib overalls, since moving sheep to the next paddock entails nothing more than clapping, whooping a bit, and walking behind the flock.

I forget about the whole lamb thing. Moving ewes to fresh grass goes smoothly because the ewes understand gates. But add 100 baby lambs to the mix, and moving sheep can be serious work.

Melissa has already moved the sheep, but two lambs have been left behind. They'd either been sleeping or off horsing around in the tall grass and not paying attention. Melissa is chasing them back and forth, trying to get them through the open gate.

Imagine a horseshoe. The flock is at one tip, and the two lambs are at the other tip. To rejoin the flock, the lambs must walk all the way around the curved end of the horseshoe to get through a gate. We try to get the lambs to do this, but they won't go. They want to go from tip to tip, but there are two electric fences in the way.

"Run!" Melissa yells to me as the two lambs scamper past me once again. I shuffle faster in my jeans, which seem to be shrinking even more as I shuffle.

"I can't!" I yell back.

We finally force them into a corner with a netted fence. One thirty-pound linebacker leaps right over the fence, but the other gets stuck in the fence right at my feet. Here's my opportunity.

"Grab him!" Melissa yells from the far side of the thistle patch. I bend over at the waist but can't bend my knees. My pants are sweaty from running and—did I mention?—a little tight. Nothing bends. "I can't," I cry as my hands flail uselessly an inch above the struggling lamb. My arms aren't long enough and I can't bend my knees. Don't even get me started on the chafing.

"Get him!" Melissa cries as she runs toward us.

"I can't!" I'm about to let myself fall on the lamb, like a denim tree being felled, when he breaks free and zooms away.

"Or you could just stand there looking good in those jeans," she says with a sigh.

"Oh, that I can do." We watch the two lambs disappear.

There is only one option left. We walk up to the main flock, where the sheep are happily munching on fresh grass. "Sorry, girls, but everyone has to go back to the old paddock." You should have seen the eyes roll. It takes major running around and yelling to convince the sheep they need to stop eating and walk back around the horseshoe into the paddock they'd just left. When they do, the two little naughties happily run to greet them. Then we have to say, "Okay, girls, now back to the new paddock." More eye rolling. It's embarrassing.

Back at the house, I'm so exhausted from chasing sheep that I bury my face in a loaf of bread. Whereas my eating habits as a tired farmer bring relief in the short term, in the long term the results have not been as beneficial.

Once I've stuffed myself in the belief that food will make me feel better, I'm still so hot and sweaty I can barely peel the jeans off. Because wool absorbs more moisture than cotton, perhaps I should have been wearing wool jeans. Or a larger size.

This Is Your
Brain on Oxytocin

Being high is one of the most pleasant sen-
sations available to mankind. Every day is
Saturday.

—JOHN ROSEVEAR

People love visiting farms. Some want to touch the animals.
Some want to emotionally touch nature. And a few just want to
touch the electric fence. In the United States in 2007, 2.8 million
sheep, about half of all the sheep in the country, lived on small
farms. Most people who've sung "Mary Had a Little Lamb" have
never actually touched one, so it's magic when they can.

More people are seeking out opportunities to experience a
farm. Gone is the old-fashioned "dude ranch" where people sat
around drinking martinis and watching others work. Today people

actually pay money to visit farms and help. There are demonstration farms where people help with lambing. Kim Severson writes in the *New York Times* of paying $300 per night to stay in a canvas tent, complete with woodstove for heating, and help put up hay for winter. Holy Frijoles. We have a tent. We'd set it up for $300.

The good news about all of this is that people are making connections. A Vermont dairy farmer with a B&B has noticed that thirty years ago, city visitors didn't pay much attention to what she did. Today's visitors want to know more about food politics, land use, and environmental stewardship. Small farms give them a place in which to learn more.

We have visitors of all ages come to our sheep farm, but hands down the most appreciative of all of them are the ten-year-olds. They soak up fascinating facts like sponges, and Melissa is filled with facts. She also has cool farm equipment.

A new acquaintance, recently come to Minnesota from New Jersey, brings her husband, her thirteen-year-old daughter, her eleven-year-old son, and her black standard poodle, Atticus, to visit. The woman and I talk, the husband keeps the neutered but enthusiastic Atticus from humping our neutered but nervous Molly, and the daughter stands in the shade simultaneously using my hula hoop and reading.

The boy has the best time of all. Melissa shows him where the hens hide their eggs, and he's able to cup his hands around a freshly laid egg, smooth and warm. He rides on the four-wheeler. He climbs into the tractor with Melissa. She fires it up and he works the controls to lift up a pile of composting soil. He visits the steers, hearing the long, mournful low of a cow for the first time. He visits the sheep and touches their wool.

If I hadn't rung the huge iron bell outside our front door, Melissa and Max would be touring the farm still. Max currently wants to be an architect and a pianist and a downhill skier. He might have been tempted to add farming to the list, but then he asks Melissa if you could make money farming. She gives him an honest answer.

Without small farms, nonfarmers—which is 99.3 percent of our population—would lose the opportunity to see animals, touch them, and meet the people who raise them. Shepherds and other small farmers don't get paid to make and keep those connections, however. They must have a product to sell, and people must buy it.

We often send visitors home with a carton of fresh eggs or a handful of peacock feathers. Whenever a family gets back into the car, a child in the group is likely holding the small piece of raw fleece Melissa has given her. She'll hold it up to the light, sniff it, and rub it against her arm, enchanted to have connected with a sheep and be taking a little part of her home.

Writer Meg Olmert offers an explanation for people's fascination with farms in her book, *Made for Each Other: The Biology of the Human-Animal Bond*: "They come in search of something they never knew but still miss. They just want to make sure that whatever 'it' was still exists."

Although chickens are the big hit with kids during farm visits, adults like the sheep. In fact, when people are interested in getting up close and personal with a sheep (in an entirely healthy and platonic and non-gross sort of way) Black Girl and White Girl are the favorites. The other sheep are too timid to approach strangers, but not these two. One particular day, Black Girl marches right up to a young woman and shoves her nose into the woman's hand in search of grain. Empty-handed, the woman offers another sort of treat. She buries her fingers in the wool along Black Girl's side and rubs.

I expect Black Girl to walk away, but instead she makes a happy grunting sound. She isn't exactly worfling, but she's coming close. When the woman reaches across Black Girl's back and begins massaging both sides, Black Girl stands perfectly still and grunts again with pleasure. The more the sheep grunts, the happier the woman is, and the longer she massages the ewe.

I need to end the tour so I can get back to my writing, but both Black Girl and the woman are in a trance. In the direct manner most Minnesotans use to confront someone not doing what they want, I say, "Well, okay, then."

This doesn't get the woman's attention so I get more aggressive. "Well, okay, then. Let's go visit the chickens."

Still the woman and Black Girl stay put, neither wanting the exchange to end. Finally I manage to break the spell and Black Girl staggers away, too blissed out to walk straight. The woman glows.

It turns out I have witnessed, right before my eyes, a little oxytocin feedback loop.

Oxytocin: the reason farmers keep farming even though animals beat them up and batter their bank accounts. It was first identified in 1902 as the hormone that acts on the muscles of the uterus to produce labor contractions. We now know it does so much more. According to Olmert, oxytocin is released into the body through a portal at the base of the brain, and scientists now believe it helps establish social attachments between mammals.

Olmert builds a credible case for the idea that oxytocin is what drew humans and animals together, and is what is keeping us together. The chemical can quiet the brain and allow us to see the world as a less threatening place. It creates strong feelings of recognition and commitment between mammals. She believes oxytocin might have been the hormone in both humans and animals that aided domestication of livestock:

> As the first farmers stroked their animals, they raised the oxytocin levels of these captured creatures, making the animals' brains, bodies and behavior calmer and more cooperative. The warmth and acceptance felt in that touch also produced a reciprocal release of oxytocin in the keepers. Just as caring for a baby releases the oxytocin that helps mothers relax into a more sedentary, repetitive lifestyle, so the nurturing aspects of domestication appear to have released a similar oxytocin effect on most of humanity.

Kerstin Uvnas-Moberg, a Swedish scientist, found that repeated exposure to oxytocin calmed very nervous rats. There were not only physiological changes such as lowered cardiovascular and stress measurements, but the rats were better able to figure out puzzles. Studies comparing nervous and calm cattle have found that calmer cattle can think more clearly and solve more puzzles. Most humans are more clearheaded when they are calm enough to reason out a problem.

Kids with ADHD were enrolled in a Pennsylvania project that allowed them to visit the zoo and "adopt" smaller animals as pets. Thanks to their interaction with the animals, the kids became calmer, more alert, and better able to listen and learn. Scientists also believe that oxytocin can bolster our immune system and protect us from infection. There's a scientific explanation why so many of us bring cats and dogs into our homes and take on the responsibility of their care: oxytocin.

Now that I know what's happening, it's fun to watch Black Girl in action. She'll stand in front of a visitor, even if there is no grain involved. People freaked out by germs won't touch an animal, but most people will reach down and pat Black Girl. She stands there, patient, until the person gets a little more vigorous with the scratching and the oxytocin feedback loop begins.

I watch her do this again and again. She's an oxytocin junkie, willing to do anything to get her fix. Watching Black Girl in action makes me realize how long it's been since I've had an "oxy" moment with one of our animals. Maybe all I need to feel better is a more regular "fix."

Or maybe I need to accept that though my life is rich with farm stories, that may not be enough. After years of shearing sheep and shipping the fleece off to the wholesalers without much thought, after years of scoffing at fiber freaks, perhaps it's time to pay more attention to the woof running through my life.

PART

THREE
Spinning Yarns

Woolology 101

A love affair with knowledge will never end in heartbreak.

—Michael Garrett Marino

As a shepherd, I've learned a great deal about sheep: how to keep them healthy, how to move them from point A to point B, how to interpret their sproings and worfls. But since our main farm product is meat, not fiber, I know almost nothing about wool itself. Perhaps my aversion to fiber freaks closed my mind to learning more. This doesn't seem fair to the sheep, or to me, so I'm unlocking the padlock, pushing open the rusty gate, and entering the Pasture of Wool . . . just to educate myself, mind you. Nothing more.

I begin my research and find my first humiliation: If you look at the inside label of nearly any wool garment, you'll see the phrase "100% Virgin Wool." Where does virgin wool come from?

As comedians like to say, "From the sheep that runs the fastest." I thought "virgin wool" came from a lamb that had never done the deed.

Wrong.

Then I thought that virgin wool was from an animal that had never been shorn before. Still embarrassing, still wrong.

It turns out that virgin wool is simply wool that has never been used for anything else, but has come straight off the sheep. Virgin wool can come from an old ewe that's been bred every year, and shorn every year. Back in the day, wool was regularly recycled and reused, so I suppose the label was developed to differentiate new wool from reused. Why didn't they say "100% New Wool"?

I think I'm allergic to wool until I read there are fewer allergies to wool than to any other known fiber. So why do over 30 percent of Americans believe they're allergic to wool? One possibility is that people with sensitive skin might be allergic to the chemicals used to wash, treat, and dye fibers of all types, including wool. For example, chemical abrasives are often used to wash raw wool for processing, and chlorine and mothproofing chemicals are routinely applied to conventional wool before turning it into a finished product. To test this idea, I hold a hunk of our untreated, unprocessed fleece against my skin. Nothing. No itching. There might be something to this.

A more likely explanation for thinking we're allergic, however, comes from wool's structure. A wool fiber is made up of overlapping scales. Imagine clay pots stacked inside each other, and you'll have the structure of a strand of wool. Some of us with sensitive skin can feel the sharp edges of those "pots," or scales.

The size of wool's scales can vary. A strand of wool is measured in microns—the lower the number, the finer the strand—and microns range from seventeen up to forty. The finer the strand, the less likely we are to feel those edges because they're so small. That's why baby blankets and soft, drapey sweaters are made from the wool of Merino sheep, or from alpacas, because that fleece has a lower micron count.

Unfortunately, clothing labels don't list the wool's micron count. But the people who buy wool for textile manufacturing know. Several years ago a 200-pound bale of 11.6 micron fleece was sold at an Australian auction for $237,000. Yowza. Wish my sheep had created that wool. According to the article in *The Shepherd*, an Indian fabric manufacturer planned to make it into about fifty likely *very* expensive men's suits.

How wool feels against our skin depends on how it has been spun. Most of the wool used in socks, sweaters, scarves, and coats has been spun into woolen yarn, which is fuzzy, with little bits sticking out. Wool spun using the worsted method is smooth. Most wool suits, pants, and skirts are worsted, and won't have the fuzzy bits.

I learn about black wool versus white wool. When we bought Andy, a large Hampshire ram with a black face and black legs, we introduced color into our flock. Soon our lambs were a riotous mix of all white, speckled, spotted, and all black. One lamb was white with a black spot on his back. Another was black with white spots on his face. Another looked just like a Dalmation. Black Girl came to be because we introduced Andy's genes into our flock.

But when he shears, Drew is adamant about keeping black or speckled fleece out of the wool bag, so we separate any fleece with black and throw it away. This isn't racism but reality. Wool with any color in it—black, brown, tan—will not take a dye in the same way as white wool. So wholesale wool buyers need all the wool to be white for quality assurance. If the end product is your burgundy wool suit, you expect the entire suit to be burgundy, not burgundy with random bits of brown or black.

For thousands of years, shepherds feared the presence of black sheep living nearby, since an accidental crossbreeding could contaminate their pure white fleece. That's the source of the phrase, "the black sheep in the family." As Jacob said to Laban in the Book of Genesis, "Let me pass through all your flock today, removing from it every speckled and spotted sheep and every black lamb." Yet as Ernest Lehman said, the wool of a black sheep is just as warm.

Wool—black or white—is a natural insulator, keeping you warm in winter and cooling you down in summer. Because it's made of those overlapping scales, it easily repels water. Wool breathes by wicking away moisture from the skin and releasing it into the air, leaving dry air and warmth near the skin. Polartec might keep you warm, but it doesn't breathe easily. Wool can absorb up to 30 percent of its weight in moisture without feeling heavy or damp, whereas cotton gets damp at 15 percent. Neither cotton nor polar fleece is warm when wet. Also, wool naturally repels mold and mildew.

And here's another thing I learn: Wool repels body odors. A cotton or polyester T-shirt will suck those smelly little molecules up like a sponge, but wool prefers not to be associated with those odors so it doesn't hook up with them. I will later put this property to the test.

Wool is durable. Lab tests show wool fibers can be bent back on themselves more than 20,000 times without breaking, Cotton breaks after 3,200 bends, silk after 1,800, and rayon (a synthetic) totally collapses after only 75. Wool resists wrinkles, and because of its natural crimp will retain its shape. It's fire retardant, unlike synthetic fabric, which happily burns when ignited because it's made from oil.

I read something amazing: The baseball gets its bounce, its distance, its life, from wool. Each professional baseball contains three layers of wool, called windings because the wool is wound around a rubber core. There are 220 *yards* of wool in one baseball.

I've played the piano since I was a kid—not well, but I still play. And now I learn that the lovely resonance of a piano happens because the hammers don't hit the piano wires directly (that would be a harpsichord). Each hammer is covered with a thick pad of felted wool. The Bacon Felt Company, near Boston, has been making the wool felt for pianos for over 175 years. They know which sheep produce the best wool for piano felts and know how to blend the fibers for an even better product. They build layers of fibers, then subject these layers to pressure, heat, and moisture. Because there are over 2,000 overlapping scales in each 25 mm of wool fiber, those scales lock together to create felt. And in case you think that there's just one kind of felt, it's clear from the Bacon Felt Company's Web site that it's more complex than that. They sell upper felts, under felts, knuckle felts, backcheck felts, key rest cushion felts, under lever frame felts, and upright piano understory felts. I have no idea what a "knuckle felt" is, but I love saying the name out loud.

Wool fills niche markets that few of us know about. There's a company less than 100 miles from me that sells skeins of wool yarn used to wick lubrication into the axle bearings of vintage (pre–World War II) railroad cars. A small company in England's Lake District mixes wool and bracken to form compost. The wool helps trap water to keep the plants hydrated, releasing a stream of nutrients over the growing season. The compost is like peat, only without the peat.

Wool insulates, breathes, absorbs, repels odors, and lasts. Suddenly I begin to regret owning anything that *isn't* wool. Unfortunately, after learning so much about this fiber, I move up higher on the Sheepishness Scale.

Turquoise Treasure

I cannot pretend to feel impartial about colors.
I rejoice with the brilliant ones and am gen-
uinely sorry for the poor browns.

—Winston Churchill

Sherry from Colorado returns to Minnesota for another round of medical appointments, this time bringing with her the yarn and roving she'd made out of our fleece. I once again meet her in Rochester.

"Feel this amazing yarn," she says, running her hands over a skein of our white yarn. I do the same, but I have no idea what she's talking about. It's yarn. Big deal.

"And this roving? I spun it up and it was a wonderful experience." It's a ball of wool. I squeeze the fuzzy roving and struggle to understand Sherry's enthusiasm. Besides, everything she says flies in the face of what we know about our wool. We've been told it's of medium quality, only good for carpeting or some other non-clothing-related use. Why does Sherry speak so highly of its crimp and its elasticity and its softness?

Might we be able to find a better market for our yarn than bagging it up and selling it wholesale? Encouraged by Sherry's enthusiasm, I find a local fiber mill and bring three bags to be converted from greasy, smelly fleece into balls of white and brown-gray roving and yarn.

The roving and yarn come back a few months later. It seems nice, but not being a knitter or spinner, what do I know? Our friend Jan knits some of the naturally colored yarn into a hat to show me what the yarn looks like. The white roving is in big round balls, so I post photos on my blog under the heading "Nice Orbs" and offer both roving and yarn up for sale. I blink, and it's gone. Huh.

The next month, a box arrives in the mail from Karen on the East Coast. Inside are two thick braids of dyed roving. I pick them up, turn them around and around, and nearly weep from the pure, raw *color*.

Some people are moved by Beethoven's *Moonlight Sonata* or a choir's rendition of Handel's "Hallelujah" chorus. Others can be sent heavenward by the smell of a lug of fresh peaches. My sensory drug of choice is color. I've been known to stand in the paint aisle of an art supply store, too mesmerized by the colors to move. One year I get so thirsty for bright yellow that I paint both the guest bathroom and guest bedroom such a bright yellow it makes people laugh when they enter. I consume turquoise, teal, royal blue, hot pink, and fuchsia like normal people consume coffee. I study Victoria Findlay's *Color: A Natural History of the Palette*. I keep my boxes of Crayola Crayons close by, even though I've pretty much moved beyond my coloring book phase.

Karen has dyed my roving blue and turquoise. I cradle the braids in my arms, lost in the turquoise. I take the braids apart, amazed at how deeply the wool has taken the dye. I want to spend time with these colors. I want to eat these colors. It takes a few days for a radical voice in my head to be heard, but I finally listen: I want to knit these colors into something, even though I don't knit.

Knitting. The activity I consider a waste of time. And even worse news? Before I can knit, I must spin the roving into yarn.

Crap. Spinning again.

I curl the braids into a basket and set them on the table. But no amount of longing looks and tender pats turns the roving into yarn.

So I dust off my spinning wheel and sign up for a two-day spinning class in the Twin Cities. I learn that yarn spun from Merino fleece is wonderfully soft but can't take much abrasion, so it doesn't wear well. I learn how to "skirt" a fleece, meaning how to take out all the bad stuff, like brittle tips and short pieces, and fleece bound up with dried manure. I learn that sheep's wool has thirteen different oils and waxes in it. I learn about Z twists and S twists, and how to fix too much of each.

I learn how to prepare a sheep's fleece for spinning. The first step is washing it. Washing wool has always been called scouring, which doesn't mean what it means today. We think of "scour" as using hard chemicals or lots of pressure to clean something, but when it comes to wool, "scour" means to wash it, not to rub hard with a Brillo pad. This would be bad, because if you apply too much pressure, you've got yourself a nice wad of felt. To clean the fleece, you use either gentle soap or stale urine, depending upon the century in which you live.

The next step is to card the wool into roving, the stuff that spinners stretch out and spin into yarn. Carding means fluffing the fleece up using wooden paddles, or cards, embedded with little metal teeth. All the students in the spinning class are provided with a pair of carders. You put a little piece of washed fleece on the teeth, then drag the cards against each other. You pull the fluff off, put it back on the teeth, then repeat the process three or four times. After a grueling hour of carding, I have a pile of carded fleece the size of a baby rabbit.

Finally it's time to spin. Even though I'd been ready to throw my wheel through the window when Kim had tried to teach me, my fingers somehow remember what to do, only this time they do it better. My yarn is thinner and not twisted as tightly. It breaks less often. The yarn is still irregular, but the thumb-sized stuff is gone. I become fascinated with how quickly the pile of roving in my lap ends up as yarn on the bobbin. I learn to take two bobbins of yarn and ply them together to create something called, not surprisingly, two-ply yarn. I spend the two days happily spinning the white roving provided in the class, but my thoughts are on the blue and turquoise.

I think about naming this turquoise yarn. When I research fiber, I learn that dyers group their dyed yarn or roving into "colorways." One Web site has a creative colorway of fairy tales, with color names like the Evil Stepmother, the Frog Prince, the Wicked Witch. Another has an entire colorway called Revenge. Each color represents a different reason for leaving your spouse, "for taking your stash and hitting the road." Another has a colorway called the Seven Deadly Skeins. Not surprisingly, the best-seller is Lust.

Fairy tales and revenge aren't working for me when it comes to this blue and turquoise roving. Of course, given my changing personality, the yarn names Cranky Bitch or Exhausted Shepherd come to mind, but the yarn is too pretty for such negativity. How about Ocean Paradise? No. Melting Mountain Stream. On a train trip west through the snowy Rockies years ago, at dusk I'd looked out of my window down into a mountain stream running right alongside the track. The water was so clean it was pure turquoise, and so deeply touched me that I teared up. Elvis was still dead.

I return home from the spinning class, set my wheel up in the living room, and begin spinning the Melting Mountain Stream. I have to stop often, not to rethread the spinning wheel or cuss at myself, but to admire what I've done. Spinning is oddly soothing, and almost mesmerizing as I watch the roving disappear into the orifice and come out yarn on the other side.

I find the idea of actually making something out of wool a little intimidating, but that's probably the fear talking. I search for easy things to make from wool and find online instructions for making wool dryer balls. Instead of using dryer sheets full of chemicals, toss the balls into the dryer and "let them bounce around to soften clothes and absorb static cling." Cool.

I keep spinning. Something weird happens. When I hold the skein of my hand-spun yarn, with all its lumps and imperfections, I'm immensely proud of our sheep.

Super Sheep

It wasn't the Exxon Valdez captain's driving
that caused the Alaskan oil spill. It was yours.
—Greenpeace advertisement,
New York Times, 1990

I wonder what role wool plays in the environment. Since wool comes from sheep, and sheep are supposedly bad for the environment, it's not looking good for wool. Ever since that UN report came out, I've been under a discouraged cloud. Yes, it's just one report, but because of it I not only feel guilty as a livestock farmer, but also as a carnivore.

Then my online news service sends me the breaking news: "UN Admits Error in Report on Global Warming." What? It turns out that an American scientist from the University of California at Davis found an error. He said that meat and milk production generate less greenhouse gas than most environmentalists claim and that the UN emissions figures were calculated differently than the transportation figures, resulting in an "apples-and-oranges analogy that truly confused the issue."

One of the authors of the UN report agreed. "I must say honestly that he has a point—we factored in everything for meat emissions, and we didn't do the same thing with transport."

It turns out that the vast majority of global greenhouse gas emissions attributed to livestock production result from deforestation and converting rain forests to grow crops or use as pasture. In the United States, only 2.8 percent of emissions come from animal agriculture, and this number has remained constant since 1990. So when it comes to greenhouse gases, we can stop pointing fingers at livestock. Sheep aren't the culprit. Hey! I'm not destroying the planet.

Yes, there are still many problems with livestock production. We eat more meat than we should, basically because we're not paying all the costs associated with it. Intensive livestock production creates more manure than the local environment can absorb. It consumes ridiculous amounts of water, something that a pasture-based system doesn't do. There are animal welfare issues.

But the animals themselves aren't the problem—it's how they're raised. Raising livestock on pasture can actually help the environment. Nicolette Niman wrote in the *New York Times* that "many smaller traditional farms and ranches in the United States have scant connection to carbon dioxide emissions because they keep their animals outdoors on pasture and make little use of machinery." And here's that carbon sink idea again: "Pasture and grassland areas used for livestock reduce global warming by acting as carbon sinks. Converting cropland to pasture, which reduces erosion, effectively sequesters significant amounts of carbon."

But how do you manage plants used as a carbon sink? Why not keep thousands of acres of land in grass to soak up carbon dioxide, then keep the grass under control using sheep? The meat and wool will be a by-product of reducing carbon dioxide in the atmosphere.

An example of what sheep mean to the landscape can be found in England's Lake District, a verdant area with lakes and breathtakingly steep green hills grazed by sheep. Experts predict profits on the sheep and cattle farms are likely to drop by up to 40 percent in the next five years. What will happen if the sheep farms disappear from northern England? Scrub and trees will replace the grass, so the land will no longer be accessible to walkers. The birds that thrive on the moors will vanish. The peatland moors also work as a carbon sink, acting as the single largest carbon reserve in the United Kingdom, storing more carbon than the woods of Britain and France combined. Without grazing sheep, shrubby vegetation will appear, dry out the peat, and release more CO_2 into the atmosphere.

After my recycling debacle, which I must confess I have repeated twice more, at least now I can take sheep off my planet-harming activities. This is a relief. If it weren't for my chronic insomnia, I'd totally be able to sleep now.

Sheep have been a good idea for 10,000 years, and they remain so because sheep (and goats) are the planet's self-propelled lawn mowers. Whether you believe God designed the sheep or that the sheep evolved over the millennia, it's still a darned smart design. The sheep is one of the most efficient machines for converting sun and water and nutrients into protein and energy, which we use in the form of meat, milk, leather, and wool. Sheep are ruminants, which means they have four chambers to their stomachs. (In case you're burning to know, other ruminants include cattle, goats, giraffes, bison, yaks, water buffalo, deer, camels, alpacas, llamas, wildebeest, antelope, pronghorns, and something called a nilgai.)

When a sheep chews a mouthful of grass and swallows it, that grass heads for the chamber called the rumen. After it's hung out there for a while and softened a bit, the sheep burps it back up and chews it a second time. That's what she's doing when she's chewing her cud. Then she swallows it again and it moves through the other three chambers where special bacteria break it down even farther. Why all the need for digestion? Many green, growing things contain lots of cellulose, which isn't digestible by humans and other monogastrics. But a ruminant's four-stage process can handle it.

Sheep are used in the United States to control invasive exotic weeds, reduce the fire risks around urban areas, and control weeds on farms without using chemicals. They eat weeds in Christmas tree farms, vineyards, national parks, along power lines, irrigation canals, and roadsides, and in forest plantations. They can be herded into roadless areas. They leave no chemical residue, just manure that breaks down and fertilizes the soil. They improve biodiversity, for if a noxious non-native weed is set back, then the native plants have the chance to recover.

Cattle won't eat leafy spurge, which crowds out all other plants and forms a monoculture. Sheep, on the other hand, love leafy spurge. When Montana and North Dakota used sheep to control leafy spurge, it cost as little as 60 cents per acre, compared to $35 per acre to spray herbicides from a helicopter.

Sheep happily munch on the kudzu taking over the southeastern United States. I *love* that the quiet, unassuming, nearly forgotten sheep can be Super Weeder, able to conquer kudzu in a single bite, or nearly so.

Alfalfa growers in California's Imperial County use 200,000 to 300,000 lambs every winter for weed control, creating the largest concentration of sheep in the nation for those months. The lambs provide both weed and insect control, cutting down on pesticide use and improving water quality.

Many urban areas are surrounded by wild brushland, a fire waiting for a spark. Sheep and goats to the rescue. California uses them to graze down highly flammable shrubs, basically creating firebreaks. In Carson City, Nevada, sheep removed 75 percent of the "fuels" around the city, and 90 percent of the citizens surveyed preferred the sheep over applying herbicides or mowing the fuel breaks. As the Carson City program proclaimed, "Only Ewes Can Prevent Wildfire."

One summer we had rain, and more rain, and more rain. Our lawn went crazy. I tried to mow, but the blade clogged so often that the mower came to a sad end and flipped over on its back, wheels pointing straight up, its headlights now little Xs.

What's a homeowner to do?

Super Sheep to the rescue. Melissa put up a temporary electric fence, then opened the big red gate and called the sheep. They leaped into the yard and scampered about, almost too excited to eat. There was even some actual sproinging. Apparently, the grass actually *is* greener on the other side.

The sheep mowed the grass down to golf course lushness, then Melissa took them out and moved them into the Bowl Pasture. The only sign the sheep did the work instead of the fuel-guzzling lawn mower were the small piles of Milk Dud–sized manure.

I may not recycle or compost consistently, but at least I raise sheep.

Now if I could just get over Elvis.

The Fuzzy Patriots

Patriotism is not short, frenzied outbursts of
emotion, but the tranquil and steady dedica-
tion of a lifetime.

—ADLAI E. STEVENSON

Sheep might be the most colorful animals on the planet. They're
green. They're covered in white or black or brown fleece. And if
you shear off that fleece, underneath you'll find centuries of red,
white, and blue.

Wool has kept U.S. soldiers warm in every war. Pioneers in
Oregon built mills and made blankets for soldiers in the Civil
War. One of the early Oregon mills is still there—Pendleton.
During World War II we couldn't produce enough wool to keep
our troops in warm uniforms and blankets, so we had to import
wool. The National Wool Act was created in 1954 to encourage

farmers to produce more wool by giving them government sub-
sidies. Today the largest buyer of U.S. wool is the U.S. military.

During the wars in Iraq and Afghanistan, soldiers beat the heat
by wearing polyester T-shirts designed to wick away moisture and
keep them dry. Unfortunately, because it's made from petroleum,
you can't get much more flammable than a synthetic T-shirt. Hidden IED explosives in Iraq have severely burned thousands of U.S.
soldiers. Add a layer of melted plastic over those burns and you
have horrific wounds.

A surgeon writes in an online issue of the *Marine Corps News*:
"Burns can kill you and they're horribly disfiguring. If you're throwing melted synthetic material on top of a burn, basically you have
a bad burn with a bunch of plastic melting into your skin and that's
not how you want to go home to your family."

That's why wool manufacturers worked with the military to design a fabric using wool's natural fire-retardant properties. They
made a blend of 50 percent wool and 50 percent aramid (a synthetic that's more flame resistant than most). "The fabric feels like
silk," said Jeanette Cardamone, a researcher at the U.S. Department of Agriculture's Ag Research Service (ARS) Eastern Re-
gional Research Center in Wyndmoor, Pennsylvania. When they
field-tested the shirts, they didn't tell the troops they were wearing
wool in case they'd automatically imagine the shirts itched.

A wool expert brought a handful of these shirts to our sheep
producers' meeting one year, and the fabric was light, soft, and
amazing. We were all given the chance to buy one, even though
we weren't in the military. I looked at the pile of light tan shirts,
colored to coordinate with desert camouflage. "Do you have anything in turquoise?" No. "Melting Mountain Stream?" Again, no.

I declined to purchase one because tan isn't my best color, which proves that I can be, on occasion, a total idiot.

Sheep not only do a great job of supporting our troops, but they also supported the American colonists. In the 1600s, British cloth was very expensive and the British put restrictions on what the colonists could and could not do when it came to wool textiles. Because colonists were producing their own wool and making their own textiles, they were buying less and less of England's textiles, which was why England wanted colonies in the first place, as a ready market for their products.

So when those American upstarts continued developing their own wool clothing industry, England passed the 1699 Wool Act, declaring that "no person may export in ships or carry by horses" to anywhere outside their own colony "any wool or woolen manufactures." If caught, the ship's captain risked forfeiture of his ship and cargo, as well as paying a £500 fine. It's been said that other punishments included chopping off the hand of someone caught transporting wool.

But our clever colonial shepherds got around this ban on transporting wool. Sheep have feet, so shepherds would walk their sheep to the textile mills, shear them there, then walk them home. Of course there was a ban on transporting wool *textiles*, but these were easier to smuggle than big bags of fleece.

The British couldn't repress colonial patriots. It became a sign of patriotism to wear clothing made from American wool. Soon even fashionable people dressed in either homespun or linsey-woolsey, a colonial mix of wool and linen or cotton. By 1763, the colonists were spinning like mad. It took about four colonial spinners to keep one weaver in yarn, which paints the picture of women being permanently attached to their spinning wheels, but still, those women were patriots.

The seed of self-sufficiency became firmly rooted in the American mind. George Washington, a sheep owner, continued this patriotic use of clothing. When he was inaugurated on April 3, 1789, he wore a suit manufactured in the new country of the United States by the Hartford Woolen Manufactory, described as "a fine, dark-brown woolen coat, waistcoat and breeches, which were worn with white silk stockings and shoes with silver buckles." For his 1809 inauguration, President James Madison wore a suit of "domestic broadcloth," woven from the wool of Vermont sheep. I wonder how long it's been since an American president has worn a wool suit made in America to his inauguration.

This idea of Americans being so determined to be self-sufficient seems overly quaint, almost laughable now, given our devotion to globalization, but it makes me sad to think it's something we may never see again. We're supposed to blindly accept globalization as inevitable, yet I wonder what would happen if patriotism became something more than waving the flag or supporting the president no matter what he did or said, and instead became a way to improve people's lives here, to support American industry, to really put our dollars where they mattered.

A few years ago sock-maker Wigwam Mills in Sheboygan, Wisconsin, decided to buy as much American wool as possible, not for patriotic reasons but for practical ones, since the company found that American wool's tighter crimp created better resilience and insulation.

Goodhew Socks in Tennessee is in the process of converting part of its sock production to an "all-domestically sourced product." This was apparently the theme of many conversations heard by wool consultants at a recent Outdoor Retailer Summer Show. Said one consultant in *Sheep Industry News*, "The demand for domestic products is growing. Everyone we talk to expresses strong desire to bring their products back to the United States and promote the fact that they are all domestic."

George Washington would be proud.

The Queen of
Do-It-Yourself

Hawkeye: Margaret, wasn't this potholder supposed to be a scarf?
Margaret: It hasn't been a scarf in weeks. I'm
knitting a sweater for a pilot I met in Tokyo.
—*M*A*S*H* (TV), 1980

After I spin two spools of my Melting Mountain Stream roving,
it's time to ply them together. The end result is stunningly beautiful. Thin threads of turquoise wind around thicker threads of
blue, then the opposite, then a stretch of mostly blue, then suddenly turquoise stripes, then heathered blue. It's so wonderfully
chaotic that it looks as if I knew what I was doing. But now what?
I must learn to knit. Spinning is fairly uncomplicated, but knitters
use a complicated language: *K1, P2*, rpt bet * across, ending K1.

I read this as *knit one, purl two, scream three*. A friend helps me "cast" the stitches onto a needle to make a practice scarf out of purchased pink yarn. I knit, purl, and scream until the scarf is long enough. Now what? I take the scarf and needles with me to my next speaking engagement, a fiber festival in Lake Elmo, Minnesota. As I open my talk, I hold up my scarf, explain my problem, and the hands fly up. The woman in the front row casts off the scarf as I talk. Obviously, I'm going to have to learn that technique myself by tiptoeing farther into the scary Do-It-Yourself forest.

I was always vaguely embarrassed by my grandmother's do-it-yourself crafts, but now I understand what she was up to. No longer ranching, she needed to do something with her hands, to produce something. She wanted to entertain us—which the Kewpie Doll Powder Dispenser certainly did—and she wanted to create something practical.

These are three guidelines I could apply in my own life: (1) Make productive use of my hands; (2) Make something beautiful; (3) Make something useful.

More and more people are discovering what my grandmother knew—that making stuff with your hands is rewarding. The Great Recession was a great help in bringing this home to people. In an effort to save money but still give holiday gifts, millions of people made their own gifts. Said the manager of an Oregon craft store, "A lot of people are doing a do-it-yourself Christmas because of the economic downturn but also wanting to make their lives more sustainable, making stuff as opposed to buying stuff." A woman in Rochester, New York, wanted to give gifts to twenty friends but didn't have a lot of cash. For about $1 apiece, she knit coffee sleeves to replace the cardboard ones from coffee shops. Each took about an hour to knit as she watched TV.

If I start doing more things with my hands, whether that's woodworking or gardening or knitting or baking cookies, I might fall into the condition made famous by the psychologist with the impossible name: Mihaly Csikszentmihalyi. That condition is "flow." It means becoming completely involved in an activity not for the sake of the outcome but for the sheer joy of it. It means feeling alive when we are fully in the groove of doing something. According to Csikszentmihalyi, the path to greatest happiness lies not with mindless consuming but with challenging ourselves to experience or produce something new, becoming in the process more engaged, connected, and alive.

Studies have found that doing things with our hands helps our mental health. It relieves stress. According to *Craft to Heal: Soothing Your Soul with Sewing, Painting, and Other Pastimes*, the repetitive motions of some activities may evoke the "relaxation response—a feeling of bodily and mental calm that's been scientifically proven to enhance health and reduce the risk of heart disease, anxiety, and depression." Learning to do something with your hands also keeps the brain sharper because we grow more dendrite connections when we learn something new.

To dive deeper into the world of do-it-yourself fiber freaks—I'm sorry, fiber *fans*—I attend an all-day working meeting of the Zumbro River Fiber Arts Guild. Thirty women and one man spend the day in the basement of the Oronoco Community Center working on their projects. People bring spinning wheels and looms and bags of knitting. I bring my spinning wheel, but then I realize I'm surrounded by people who know how to knit, and I'm itching to knit my Melting Mountain Stream into something.

I befriend a young woman to my right who shows me how to cast on, which means putting the first row of stitches on the needle. I feel like a ten-fingered tree sloth, but finally get the hang of it. All goes well until I get too involved in the conversation around me and suddenly look down, having created a fearful snaggle of something. The woman on my left is one of those irritating people who'd rather *teach* you how to solve the problem than just fix it. She walks me through undoing the mess.

At the end of the day, the organization's president has us go around the room and show off our projects. Carolyn is knitting a burgundy sweater full of cables. Lori shows off a sweater exploding with purple and pink. Judy displays a complicated scarf she's woven. Robert holds up a brightly colored table runner.

When my turn comes, I hold up my knitting needles. "I have knit this rectangle."

The crowd goes wild. I feel silly and proud at the same time. These fiber people are so encouraging that I want to keep at this, to figure it out. I have plans to turn the rectangle into a wrist warmer, but that's about it for my knitting goals. Besides, spinning is fun now that I can sort of do it, and it feels basic, a connection with spinners stretching back into the past. I'm rediscovering my colonial roots.

Of course, at the rate I'm learning, I see that if most of us had to rely on our own skills to make our own clothing, our fashion expectations would change radically. The rectangle, formerly known as the loincloth, would make a rapid comeback.

Greener Than You Think

The key to saving the environment is not recycling. As Thoreau so wisely noted, we must strike at the root, not hack at the branches.

—Tere Saudavel

Now that I know I'm not destroying the planet by raising sheep, I look into the environmental, political, and social aspects of wool and its "competitors," cotton and synthetics. After a week of googling my fingers to the first knuckle, I decide the only way to avoid causing *any* environmental or political or social damage with my clothing choices is to forgo even the loincloth and go buck naked. My instinct is to drop the whole subject and not think about it. If I can't bear to schlep the recycling into town, what am I doing paying attention to my clothing?

Cotton is the most-produced, most widely used fiber on the planet. Out of the annual world production of natural fibers of 30 million tons, 20 million are cotton. Jute comes in at 3 million tons, and wool is third at 2 million tons.

Cotton uses more than 25 percent of all the insecticides in the world, and 21 percent of all the herbicides, yet cotton is farmed on only 3 percent of the world's farmland. The pesticides and synthetic, oil-based fertilizers often end up in groundwater, surface water, and our drinking water. In 1995, pesticide-contaminated runoff from cotton fields in Alabama killed 240,000 fish. Twelve of the top fifteen cotton pesticides in California caused birth defects, ten caused multiple birth defects, and thirteen were toxic or very toxic to fish or birds or both. According to the U.S. Environmental Protection Agency, seven of the top fifteen pesticides used on cotton in the United States are considered "possible," "likely," "probable," or "known" human carcinogens.

The U.S. cotton industry has reduced its use of chemicals, but how many of us buy cotton clothing from other countries? The Environmental Justice Foundation advises people to "pick your cotton carefully," since in many developing countries cotton involves child labor, rampant use of pesticides, and using too much water. I was shocked to see the photos of the Aral Sea in Central Asia, which has become a desert because two rivers were diverted to water cotton fields.

During cotton harvest, producers apply herbicides to defoliate the plants to make picking easier. Then to convert cotton into something soft enough for us to wear, it must be chemically processed. After it's washed, cotton fiber is coated with polyvinyl alcohol sizing to make it easier to weave. After it's woven, it's bleached. Then the sizing is removed with a detergent. Then it's washed with sodium hydroxide.

The cotton story keeps getting worse. The final step for most cotton garments, those easy-care clothes that are soft, wrinkle-resistant, stain- and odor-resistant is "finishing." Any fabric or clothing labeled static-resistant, wrinkle-resistant, permanent-press, no-iron, stain-proof, or moth-repellent likely includes some synthetic fiber or is a natural fiber that's been coated with a chemical. Farmers can't plant wrinkle-free cotton. To make it wrinkle free, the fabric has been treated. Chemicals used in finishing often cause allergic reactions and include "formaldehyde, caustic soda, sulfuric acid, bromines, urea resins, sulfonamides, and halogens." Some imported cotton clothes are now impregnated with long-lasting disinfectants that are hard to remove. That explains the two cotton shirts I bought for only $15 apiece. They were fine until I washed them. Now they smell permanently like bug spray and are unwearable.

All this news about cotton makes me sad. I thought cotton was a clean, pure product. Organic cotton is of course an option, but I've noticed it's not readily available in a wide range of colors. In fact, it's as if the organic cotton mills think people who care about the planet only look good in cream, taupe, and pale green. Where's the bright turquoise organic T-shirt? Maybe organic dye doesn't come in turquoise, or fuchsia, or screaming yellow.

I'm a little horrified at what goes into growing and processing cotton. In fact, if you compare raising sheep with growing cotton, wool looks pretty good. Raising sheep for wool, if done well, uses minuscule amounts of pesticides and herbicides. You don't need to kill weeds in a pasture because sheep will eat them. How great is that?

I've decided to continue wearing cotton, but I resolve to find ways to replace a cotton garment with wool. I wonder if anyone makes wool underwear.

Wool's other "competitor" is synthetic fabric. Most synthetics are made from chemicals. Most chemicals are made from petroleum. That's right. Bubbling crude. Oil, that is. Black gold. Texas tea.

A few synthetic fibers come from renewable resources. Tencel and rayon both come from tree pulp. But otherwise, synthetics are made out of oil. The oil is used to make chemicals, then the chemicals are combined in creative ways and extruded through tiny holes to create threads. Remember those little Play-Doh factories where you could put different-sized holes over the opening, pressed down on the handle, and out came a long slender snake of Play-Doh? This is how synthetic fibers are made. Then these tiny strands of plastic are woven or knit into fabric. It's plastic fabric.

Synthetics go by lots of names: acetate, acrylic, modacrylic, nylon, olefin, polyester, and the latest, microfiber. The demand for synthetic fiber, especially polyester, has doubled in the last fifteen years. Why is this bad? An article in *Environmental Health Perspectives* spells it out:

The manufacture of polyester and other synthetic fabrics is an energy-intensive process requiring large amounts of crude oil and releasing emissions including volatile organic compounds, particulate matter, and acid gases such as hydrogen chloride, all of which can cause or aggravate respiratory disease. Volatile monomers, solvents and other by-products of polyester production are emitted in the wastewater. The EPA, under the Resource Conservation and Recovery Act, considers many textile manufacturing facilities to be hazardous waste generators.

Although the idea that we're using valuable resources to make *new* plastic fiber still strikes me as wrong, there might be a place for synthetic clothing made from recycled plastic. I could live with this, and some companies are doing this. However, 70 percent of America's plastic water bottles still aren't recycled (I should probably take

a wee bit of responsibility for this), so we have lots of room for im-
provement. And if we can create plastic clothes out of oil, can't we
figure out how to replace these fabrics by expanding the list of uses
for wool? Lightweight shirts, lightweight jackets, polo shirts, vests,
sweatshirts—they could all be made of wool. If we can put humans
on the moon and land little rovers on Mars and photograph the
rings of Saturn, you'd think we could come up with more environmentally friendly clothing.

Polartec is finally catching on to the wonders of wool. According to a *Sheep Industry News* article, the company is creating a product that is 44 percent wool, and the wool is 100 percent American
raised. Said a representative of Polartec, "We just really like the
U.S. wool story."

And what *about* comfortable wool undies? Why don't we give
them a try? I finally mention this to Melissa, who looks at her
crazy wife and says, "You first."

I think it's such a great idea. Do we really need oil-based synthetic underwear? Or cotton underwear? The earth "created" oil
millions of years ago, but oil is not renewable. When it's gone, it's
gone. Cotton is a renewable resource, but current production
methods harm the planet. Yet with a little help from sheep, we
could make wool underwear forever, and without high chemical
or pesticide use.

I know the world isn't so black and white that it comes down
to people choosing among cotton, plastic, and wool. We'll all
likely continue wearing cotton and plastic, but if we can replace
those fabrics with wool, it seems the planet-friendly thing to do.

I'm finding wool so inspiring that it occurs to me: Perhaps I
should give those compact fluorescent light bulbs another try.

And Photogenic,
to Boot

Kathryn Dun's *Beautiful Sheep: Portraits of Champion Breeds* provides the sheep "addicts" of the world with more than a hundred dazzling pages of wooly heroin.

—*Wild Fiber* MAGAZINE

Giving yet another farm tour, I stand at the edge of the winter feeding area, called the Sacrifice Lot because we sacrifice the grass there. Visitors watch the sheep, and I'm proud of how plump and content the sheep look. They lift their heads and watch us. Sheep can recognize up to 100 human faces, and because they've never seen the people with me, they keep their distance.

The woman and her husband are there to pick up their order of lamb. She tips her head and asks, "What breed are your sheep?" She

asks this as if confident she'll recognize it. In another fit of crankiness, I'm tempted to answer, "Jabberwocky sheep," or "Sparkle-
Farkle sheep."

Instead, I take a deep breath and rattle off our five-way mix of
breeds: "Corriedale, Columbia, Targhee, Dorset, and Finn, with a
little bit of Texel and Shropshire thrown in."

"Oh," is her answer. That is always the answer.

Most people recognize many dog breeds, some cat breeds, and
a few nonfarmers can tell a Holstein from a Scottish Highland, but
who knows what a Blue-faced Leicester looks like? Or a Babydoll
Southdown? Or a Zwartbles, or a Balwen Welsh Mountain? There
are more breeds of sheep than of any other domestic livestock
mammal. I don't know what this says about shepherds—that we
like to tinker with genetics? That we're always in search of the perfect sheep?

Maybe we are. Which sheep produces the best meat? The best
wool? Merino sheep were the gold standard of sheep in the Middle
Ages, thanks to fine wool that could be spun and woven into a
soft, supple fabric. Merinos are so wrinkly they look like huge Shar
Pei dogs with a seven-inch-long fleece. If you joined the fiber of
five Merino sheep end to end, you could wrap a thread of wool
around the world.

The Merino was developed mostly in Spain, thanks to the
sheep brought by the Moors when they controlled the Iberian
Peninsula for nearly 700 years. By the 1550s, Merino sheep were
so valuable and desired that the Spanish kings refused to sell or
trade them. Smuggling a Merino out of Spain was punishable by
death, and breeding secrets were national treasures.

The ideas of "Merino" and "Spain" became so closely woven
that soon no one was able to see them clearly. Spaniards became

convinced that the Merino sheep could only survive in Spain, that once moved from the pastures of the Iberian Peninsula, away from the tender loving care of Spanish shepherds, the sad, wrinkly sheep would die.

This gave King Philip V an idea. Why not use Merinos to pay off foreign debts or to pay required dowries to other countries? The king would get rid of his debts, but the sheep would die, leaving the recipient nothing but the realization he'd been duped. So King Philip did just that, sending the valuable Merino out into the world.

Funny thing happened. The sheep didn't die. They thrived on French pasture. They did just fine being cared for by German or Russian shepherds, and as sheep are wont to do, those lusty Merinos began reproducing. No longer was the Merino solely found in Spain.

In 1797, the Merinos reached Australia when a Dutch commandant committed suicide in Cape Town, South Africa, leaving behind a ship stocked with valuables, including thirteen of the world's finest merino sheep. His widow, not knowing their value, sold them to a ship captain who brought them to Australia, intending to sell them to the prisons for meat. Fortunately, a clever captain, John Macarthur, recognized the sheep for what they were, bought them at a ridiculously low price, and started the industry that became Australia's largest export.

In 1808, President Thomas Jefferson wrote Washington Irving, the American ambassador to Spain, hoping to snag a few Merinos because "we desire to emancipate ourselves from dependence on foreign wool." Irving came through and two years later 4,000 Merinos crossed the ocean. A handful of them ended up on Thomas Jefferson's farm. By 1810, Merino Mania was in full swing as breeders throughout the world raced to import or steal as many Merinos as possible.

The Merinos were quite expensive, not only because they'd been transported across the ocean from Europe, but because they were scarce, so the prices of these lovely animals shot through the roof. They often sold for over $1,000 apiece, which back then was a fortune. Even today, few small shepherds will pay $1,000 for a ram.

Mr. William Foster of Boston smuggled three sheep from Spain into America in 1793, and left them with a close friend of his, Andrew Craigie of Cambridge. William was going to breed these sheep and make a fortune on the fine wool he'd produce, as well as selling the offspring as breeding stock.

I can't resist imagining possible conversations William and Andrew might have had. One version could have been: "Andrew, here are three sheep from Spain. They're worth about $1,000 apiece. Could you take good care of them? They're Merino sheep which I will use to entirely transform the wool and textile industry in America. I'll be back for them. Thanks, buddy."

Or did the conversation go something like this: "Andrew, here are three sheep. Thanks, buddy." Or was there no conversation at all, but instead, did William ship them to Andrew without saying a word, thinking the guy would recognize this famous, distinctive breed and know the score?

I suspect the two never spoke. One day Andrew sent a nice little note to William, thanking him for the "thoughtful gift of mutton." Turns out he needed meat to feed his family, so he butchered William Foster's delicious plan to breed Merino sheep and carved it up on his dinner table.

Thomas Jefferson was initially so excited about the Merino that he planned to raise a huge flock and donate a ram to every county in Virginia. But eventually the tone of his letters changed when he was discussing the Merino, until he wrote, "the Merino fever has so entirely subsided in this part of the country that the farmers now will not accept of them." The Merino fleece proved to be too fine for the coarse, more durable clothing the Americans required. So the Merino wasn't going to be the perfect sheep for America.

Shepherds love tinkering with different breeds. There's an adorable gray-and-white breed, the Herdwick sheep, found in England's Lake District, which had been championed years ago by an artist and writer named Mrs. William Heelis. She bought land and filled it with Herdwicks, and in 1924 was one of the few women in the Herdwick Sheep Breeders' Association. Earlier in her life, Mrs. Heelis had written a few little books under her pen name, Beatrix Potter.

All sheep breeds have four legs and a body, but that's where the similarities stop. Some have no horns, some have two horns, some have four. Some have open faces, meaning the wool stops at the top of the head, leaving the face covered by short hair, like a dog's. Wooled faces have wool coming down to the eyes, sometimes with one curly lock dangling down over the eyes, à la Michael Jackson. Sometimes wool comes up around the cheeks as well, which is why very long sideburns on men are called "muttonchops."

Some sheep ears point straight up, others straight out. Sheep fleece comes in every shade of white, every shade of brown or black, and a few reds. Fleece can be solid or patterned. And because sheep have horizontal pupils, it's intriguing to look them in the eye. (As long as they feel safe—there's that whole "predator/prey" thing.)

Not only is wool better for the planet than plastic or cotton clothing, but it's the only fiber with a delightfully photogenic source. No one can get enough cute lamb photos. Regardless of the breed or age, sheepish people know that all sheep are lovely.

Few, however, are as lovely as a certain mix of Corriedale, Columbia, Targhee, Dorset, and Finn, with a little bit of Texel and Shropshire thrown in.

Of Warp and Woof

We sleep, but the loom of life never stops, and the pattern which was weaving when the sun went down is weaving when it comes up in the morning.

—HENRY WARD BEECHER

I continue to knit, and I have worked my way up to a simple ribbed pattern. Unfortunately, I'm still knitting wrist warmers and scarves. I've knit wrist warmers for my mom. I've knit wrist warmers and a scarf for myself. I even knit wrist warmers for my sister, who lives in Florida, which tells you I'm running out of things to knit. Because I'm still not convinced knitting is for me, I investigate weaving.

Weaving has been defined as the art by which threads are crossed and interlaced. It was done with reeds and plant materials long before wool yarn appeared on the scene. Material can be woven with nothing but your hands, or you can use looms ranging from a hunk of cardboard to a box you set on your table to one as large as your bedroom.

The big looms, with complicated threading and moving parts that bang and shift and create cloth, were mysterious and I didn't really understand how weaving worked. So I signed up for a "Give It a Try" workshop at the Weavers Guild in the Twin Cities. The class description promised we'd each weave an entire scarf in a five-hour class. I was skeptical.

Part of the reason the instructor could make this claim was because she warped the looms for her students, which saved us six hours' work and many tears, if we'd had to do it ourselves. I was the first to arrive, so I was able to choose the loom I wanted to use. I zeroed right in on the loom with the purple and fuchsia and blue warping. The loom was called a Baby Wolf, which for a shepherd might be a frightening thing, but I fell in love with it almost immediately.

After a few hours of instruction, we were all sitting at our looms, happily weaving. It's sort of like that old walking, chewing gum, and rubbing your stomach exercise. First you depress a treadle (pedal) that raises the harnesses that hold odd-numbered threads of the warp. Then, smoothly and without dropping it, you slide the shuttle, which contains the thread for the woof (or weft) under the odd-numbered threads and out the other side. Then you pull the beater forward, which is fitted with a reed, basically a metal comb that snugs the weft thread up to the previous row. Then you freeze, let up on the treadle, then push down the one that raises the even-numbered threads. You shift back the beater, slide the shuttle under the even threads, pull the beater forward to snug up the thread, then use your feet to lower one harness and raise the other.

I found I could do this only if I chanted to myself "down, through, snug, down, up, through, snug." We were encouraged to change woof threads often, being bold with our colors, and to *not* create a pattern like five rows of red, seventeen of blue, three of green. "Be random," the instructor exhorted.

No amount of exhortation from a short, slender woman is going to convince me to go random. After weaving six colors, I looked at what I had, loved it, and found myself back at the first color again. Why ignore a perfectly lovely pattern? The act of throwing the shuttle under the threads became hypnotic. The sound of the harnesses clattering up and down was exciting. By the end of the five hours, I had a sixty-inch beautiful scarf that I'd woven myself.

I could easily get hooked on weaving. Of course, since the Baby Wolf sells for $1,500, I won't be getting into this anytime soon. But it's incredibly exciting to have actually created fabric. I used a machine that can't be much different from the looms used by weavers 5,000 years ago. There's a weird sense of power in this. If China were to fall into the ocean and could no longer make my clothing, I feel a little better able to do it myself.

The last step is to take the scarf home and "full" it. This is the step that turns the loosely woven, stiff fabric into something soft and fluid using heat and moisture. With hot water and a little soap, I agitate the scarf until the threads tighten up, closing the gaps in the fabric. The fabric becomes soft and fuzzy, with a nap.

For thousands of years this was done by hand, which doesn't seem hard when fulling a little scarf, but it must have been back-breaking when dealing with yards and yards of fabric. When someone figured out a way to use water mills for fulling, London banned them because fulling had always been done by hand, and to use water energy would deprive fullers of work. Ancient methods of fulling involved walking on the wet cloth, so fullers were sometimes called walkers. If your last name is Fuller or Walker, this is likely what your ancestors did for a living.

Women are brilliant at turning hard work into a social gathering. In 1774, Thomas Pennant came across a group of Scottish
women walking cloth: "Twelve women sit down on each side of a
long board ribbed lengthways, placing the cloth on it; first they
begin to work it backwards and forwards with their hands, singing
at the same time; when they have tired their hands every female
uses her feet for the same purpose, and six or seven pairs of naked
feet are in the most violent agitation working one against the
other and by this time they grow very earnest in their labours, so
the fury of the song rises."

What a great idea. Instead of today's teenagers getting their
"exercise" by making four entire circuits of the Mall of America
in an afternoon, why not harness that energy by having them take
off their shoes, sing Britney Spears songs, and mush wet wool fabric around with their feet?

My scarf is fulled and dry. Anyone who comes into the house
is immediately shown the scarf. "I made this," I say. Why doesn't
everyone weave scarves? It's so satisfying. Even Melissa is impressed, and she takes take the class herself a few months later.

I seem to like this fiber world much more than I thought I
would. I've played around with having a few of our fleeces turned
into yarn and roving, but I want more.

I continue to knit because it's so portable, and soon I have
enough scarves to keep Canada warm all winter. I begin lurking in
the magazine shelves of the library, reading back issues of *Spin-Off*
and *Vogue Knitting*, finding colorful yarn or a cute sweater pattern.
A friend notices the book I'm reading, *The History of Wool*, and
snorts, "Oh, I'll bet that's a real page-turner."

Well, actually, it is.

Counting Bed Mites

Our Lord said, "Feed my sheep"; he did not say,
"Count them."

—DORA CHAPLIN

Shepherds are obsessive about counting everything—pounds of wool sheared, pounds of hay fed, number of straw bales used, percentage of lambs that survive—but most of all, shepherds count sheep.

Melissa and I started with fifty ewes. Then we had sixty, then seventy-five, then sixty, then forty-five, then fifty. As it should, our farm has a swinging gate where sheep are concerned. They're born here. Some die, some are sold. But we keep a close count on the number of ewes in our flock because when shepherds meet each other, the standard question is: How many sheep do you have?

We're all advised to count sheep as a cure for insomnia. Two Harvard psychologists in the 1970s determined that we've been given this advice because counting sheep occupies both hemispheres of the brain simultaneously, thus preventing the brain activity that's responsible for insomnia. Melissa has a cartoon in her office of a man with a clipboard standing in a pasture of sheep. His van says "Official Sheep Census." Midcount, the man has fallen asleep.

But why count sheep? Why not count chickens or pigs? Is it some sort of "sheep are boring" misconception?

Counting sheep is actually very hard to do because they look alike and tend to mill about. You start counting heads but some lower those heads to graze. You switch to counting backs but they're moving and shifting and looking very much alike. And if they start running, forget it. So, as an experienced shepherd I can't recommend counting sheep as a cure for insomnia.

If we, as a culture, insist on counting sheep, perhaps we should use the Celtic sheep-counting system that E. B. White shared in *One Man's Meat*. Here's how to count fifteen sheep:

1. Yain
2. Tain
3. Eddero
4. Peddero
5. Pitts
6. Tayter
7. Later
8. Overro
9. Covvero
10. Dix
11. Yain-dix
12. Tain-dix

13. Eddero-dix
14. Peddero-dix
15. Bumfitt

You could use it to remember codes. "My debit card PIN is Dix, Pitts, Peddero-Dix. My Facebook password starts with Eddero and ends with Bumfitt." You've got to love a system that gives you the opportunity to say the word "Bumfitt."

Sheep *can* actually help us sleep, but not by counting. It's the wool. Sleep happens with wool. Wool mattresses, pillows, blankets, and comforters draw moisture away from you as you sleep, keeping you cooler and drier than products made from synthetics, goose down, or cotton. During sleep you can lose more than one pint of water each night through your skin and breath. Studies show sleeping under wool-filled comforters lowers heart rates, suggesting a more restful sleep than with acrylic or down comforters.

And here's the kicker: Read *The Secret House: The Extraordinary Science of an Ordinary Day* by David Bodanis and you'll surround yourself with wool. You'll make a cocoon in your bed and never leave it. Apparently, our homes are filled with microscopic dust mites: "Male mites and female mites and baby mites and even, crunched to the side away from the main conglomerations, the mummified corpses of long-dead old great grandparent mites." Mites eat the dead skin that flakes off our bodies. Some people are sensitive to the, ahh, fecal matter that mites produce. According to Bodanis, the mites are so small that a huge pile of said fecal matter could fit on the period at the end of this sentence, which makes me not want to end the sentence because then I'll have the image of a tower of dung punctuating my thoughts, but I'm not sure how long I can put this off so here it is, the end of the sentence. Gross.

These mites live in our beds, about 42,000 per ounce of mattress dust, or about 2 million total in the average double bed. The mites love polyester because it traps your perspiration and they like moisture. They love down pillows and down comforters because there are so many wonderful places in which to hang out.

Counting dust mites *certainly* won't help you sleep, so what's a sleeper to do? It turns out dust mites don't like wool because wool wicks away moisture and dries out more quickly than synthetic or down. It turns out that the lanolin in wool actually *repels* dust mites.

Now and then a smart lamb will demonstrate the idea that sleep goes better with wool by climbing up onto its mother's back and settling down in the thick fleece for the best nap ever.

Inspired by this, Melissa and I buy a wool mattress made by a company ninety miles away. We have some of our wool turned into comforters and pillows. After two nights on my new wool pillow I decide I'm not going to sell the other pillows to customers because I want them all for myself.

Plus, I sleep better knowing those creepy little mites aren't defecating directly beneath my head.

A Recipe for
Carpal Tunnel

Any sufficiently advanced technology is indis-
tinguishable from magic.

—Arthur C. Clarke

I decide I should attempt to go through the entire fiber process,
fleece to yarn, all by myself. Why? I wish I knew.

So I soak a fleece in the washing machine, then spin out the
water. I lay it outside in the sun to dry. The result is six paper grocery bags overflowing with fleece. Then I buy myself a pair of
carders and begin the scritch-scritch-scratch of carding. My wrists
hurt but I keep going, determined to take one of our sheep's fleece
all the way through to a finished product. I card while I watch
DVDs. After a few months, I've barely made a dent in the six
grocery bags, and my wrists still hurt. This may take longer than I

thought. But when I finish carding, then I can spin the yarn, and then I can knit it.

My knitting has advanced to the point where I can now start and end the project myself, and feel very clever in doing so. When my aunt and uncle visit, I discover that my aunt knits as well, so I begin ranting about wool yarn, thinking we'll share a knitting bond. My dear aunt smiles ruefully. "I only knit with acrylic. It's cheaper than wool."

The world crashes around my ears. I love this woman. She was raised on that sheep ranch with my mom. She has several degrees in home economics. She's environmentally conscious. Yet she knits with acrylic yarn. Plastic yarn. A sacrilege.

I give my aunt a dressing-down for knitting with acrylic instead of wool, especially since I know she can afford wool. Then I begin sneering at friends' Polartec jackets. At one writing retreat, I look around the room. Of the fourteen women there, half are wearing polar fleece. I'm so frustrated. Why isn't everyone wearing wool? Converts are the most zealous, whether it's smoking, or drinking, or being enthusiastic about wool.

Eventually I realize that I'm turning into a fabric Nazi, judging people because they aren't avoiding plastic clothing. I myself own two polar fleece jackets, but I don't wear them in public. They are a dark secret hidden in my closet.

Wendell Berry helps me see reason in his essay "Getting Along with Nature." He wrote that while there may be two sides to a conflict, neither are absolutely right, nor should they be. He wrote of the conflict between coyotes and sheep:

The coyote-defenders may find it easy to forget that the sheep ranchers are human beings with some authentic complaints against coyotes, and the sheep-defenders find it easy to sound as if they advocate the total eradication of both coyotes and conservationists. . . . The fact is that people need both coyotes and sheep. . . . This sort of conflict, then, does not suggest the possibility of victory so much as it suggests the possibility of a compromise—some kind of peace, even an alliance, between the domestic and the wild.

Sigh. The same might be true of wool and plastic clothing.

As I card and card and card, I learn that a distant cousin in Montana has recently begun operating a small fiber mill. Perhaps I should send some business her way. I pack more fleece into five black plastic bags and ask my visiting aunt and uncle to drop them at the fiber mill when they return to Montana.

Meanwhile, I continue to card my six grocery bags full of fleece. After a few more months, the sound of the wire teeth on my carding combs rasping, rasping, rasping against each other is rasping my brain to shreds. I cannot card one more *micron* of fleece. Screw the idea of doing it all by hand. How insane.

Time to move from the "totally by hand" method to the "partially by hand" method. I pack up my grocery bags, call my friend Kathy for moral and carding support, and meet her at the Weavers Guild, where, as a member, I can use the drum carders.

A drum carder sits on a table. It's a wooden frame that holds a tray, a smallish cylinder covered in nasty little wires, and a large cylinder covered in the same stuff. Fluff up a handful of fleece, place it on the tray, then start turning the hand crank. Move the fleece forward until the little cylinder snags the fleece and feeds it onto the big cylinder. Do this a few times and soon the big cylinder is covered with fluffy, carded roving. Magic. This machine, advanced technology compared to my hand carders, is powered only by human muscle.

As I set up the drum carders, I feel a little guilty, as if I'm somehow cheating by taking this shortcut. I doubt my colonial ancestors had drum carders. Kathy shows up and we begin. We talk and crank and create fluffy batts that are about ten inches wide by eighteen inches long.

It's hard work standing there all day, but having a friend help makes all the difference in the world. It doesn't occur to me until later but we are doing exactly what women have done for ages—being productive with our hands while catching up with each others' lives, telling stories, and making each other laugh. These are benefits of do-it-yourself that I can't get from buying a sweater in the department store. After three hours of carding (six "woman" hours), we're done. Shortcuts totally rule.

Now that the carding is done, I can freely spin. I spin while my tea is steeping. I spin while waiting for Melissa. I spin before I go to bed at night. It's oddly relaxing and stress reducing, and I love seeing those bobbins fill up with yarn from our sheep. It seems that I've moved beyond the martyr Saint Catherine's fate. The spinning wheel isn't the instrument of my destruction, but of something much different.

The Stealthy Flock

> When one tugs at a single thing in nature, he
> finds it attached to the rest of the world.
>
> —JOHN MUIR

We love the Minnesota State Fair, where Melissa and I have volunteered at the Grape Growers booth, visited all the animal barns, ridden the overhead tram, and eaten way too much food on a stick. But then we add something new: Melissa and I will take a shift staffing the Baa Booth in the Sheep Building. The pork producers have the Oink Booth. The cattle building is filled with displays explaining the beef and dairy industries. And now the Sheep Building has the Baa Booth. But do we know enough about sheep to answer people's questions? I can explain what virgin wool is, but can I do much more?

The Baa Booth was built by a hardworking family that raises sheep and brings them to the fair to show them. The booth displays the cuts of meat one gets from a sheep and provides handouts listing products made from sheep. Fabric samples illustrate the difference between worsted and woolen fabrics. Here's where I'm reminded that woolen is sort of fuzzy, like a wool coat, whereas worsted has a smoother, harder finish, like a business suit. A raw fleece is spread out across a table so people can sink their fingers into it, with a bottle of hand cleaner provided. A live sheep and her lambs snooze in a nearby pen.

Spending a few hours there seems the least we can do to support sheep. For those few hours, the booth has something not found anywhere else at the Minnesota State Fair: Melissa. As I've begun learning more about wool and yarn, I've been entertaining her with the facts, and they stick in that encyclopedic brain of hers. She, too, is beginning to appreciate the fluffy stuff we've been ignoring all these years.

She also isn't shy. She draws people in and encourages them to feel the fleece. She shows people the different types of fleece—coarse, medium, and fine—and explains how each is used. I hang back, nursing a Diet Coke, but Melissa's so excited to be talking about wool that I love watching her in action. Four middle-aged women wander by and one makes the mistake of smiling at Melissa. Soon they have their hands in fleece. Then Melissa pulls them deeper into the booth and has them touching the army T-shirt on exhibit, which the booth builders had been smart enough to purchase when they had the chance. The women are fascinated, nodding at all they're learning. They've been using wool, or some part of the sheep, every day, but didn't know it.

They don't know about the baseball, or about the piano. They don't know about the insulation. Wool does a great job of insulating our bodies, so why not our houses? Builders are finally catching on, installing insulation made from 100-percent-recycled wool or a wool-polyester mix. Wool works well because of its ability to absorb and release water vapor. Wool is naturally flame retardant. Studies in Japan show that wool can absorb formaldehyde, a chemical used in the manufacturing of some building materials, including timber glue.

And then there's always wearing wool to save energy. As President Jimmy Carter recommended years ago: Turn down the heat and put on a sweater. A European commission has estimated that a household could cut its CO_2 emissions by up to 300 kg (661 pounds) a year and cut its energy bill by 5 to 10 percent by turning the thermostat down one degree.

Wool has been mixed with wood chips to form a garden mulch, cleverly called Woolch. A company in Texas sells material made from wool to clean up oil spills. The stuff absorbs more than polypropylene and can float on top of water, and you can squeeze the oil out and reuse the wool up to eight times. Wool is in your carpeting, in your carpet pads, in your magnificent rugs. Felted wool is installed inside car doors for sound insulation, put on pool tables, used to pad saddles and ballet toe shoes, and it lines gloves and fluid filters. If you use a felt eraser or felt-tip pen, it's probably made of wool.

Lanolin, the grease removed from wool, is used in adhesive tape, printing inks, motor oils, and auto lubrication. It's refined even more and used in cosmetics and pharmaceuticals. Lipstick, mascara, lotion, shampoo, hair conditioners—you name it. Yes, you're wearing a bit of sheep on your lips. Lanolin makes your skin smooth and soft. Sink your hands into the wool on a sheep's back, and they'll come out softer, smoother. You could also try sinking your face into the sheep's back for the same effect, but I can see some problems with this.

The four women spend over fifteen minutes under Melissa's spell. When she finally releases them, I hear one comment to the other as they walk away. "Wow. I had no idea sheep and wool were so important."

Melissa and I high-five each other. Four people converted, 300 million left to go. Every day, stealthy sheep are reaching out their dainty little hooves and weaving themselves into people's lives, even those people who live in huge cities and never wear wool and think sheep have nothing to do with them.*

*__Products Made from Sheep__: **Hide and Wool**: lanolin, clothing, drum heads, yarns, artists' brushes, sports equipment, fabrics and textiles, pelt products, rouge base, insulation, rug pads, asphalt binder, ointment base, tennis balls, felt, carpet, footwear, baseballs, paint and plaster binder, hospital bed pads, chamois skins for polishing, boot liners, auto seat covers, leather upholstery. **From Fats and Fatty Acids:** explosives, solvents, chewing gum, paints, rennet for cheese, industrial oils, industrial lubricants, stearic acid, cosmetics, dog food, mink oil, oleomargarine, ceramics, medicines, dish soap, tires, paraffin, chicken feed, biodegradable detergents, antifreeze, crayons, floor wax, tallow for tanning, rubber products, insecticides, candles, herbicides, shaving cream, hair conditioner and shampoo, cough medicine, insulin, creams and lotions, glycerin. **From Intestines**: sausage casings, instrument strings, surgical sutures, tennis racquet strings. **From Manure:** nitrogen fertilizer, potash, phosphorus, minerals. **From the Bones, Horns, and Hooves:** syringes, gelatin desserts, rose food, piano keys, marshmallows, pet food ingredients, bandage strips, adhesive tape, combs and toothbrushes, buttons, wallpaper and wallpaper paste, ice cream, laminated wood products, collagen and bone for plastic surgery, abrasives, bone china, dog biscuits, steel ball bearings, malts and shakes, fertilizer, plywood and paneling, shampoo and conditioner, collagen cold cream, crochet needles, cellophane wrap and tape, glycerine. *Source:* American Sheep Industry Association.

Re-cycle. Re-create.
Re-enjoy.

Veni, Vidi, Velcro. I came, I saw, I stuck around.

—AUTHOR UNKNOWN

One morning I stash our winter gear to make room for summer-weight work gloves, and for the first time I really pay attention to the pair of wool mittens Mom had given me for Christmas. The backs are patterned, the palms are a coordinating color, and the wrists are another color. They're made from recycled wool sweaters and coats that some creative person took apart and put back to-gether as another usable item of clothing.

In fact, I see now that the wool has been felted. Wool, because of those little scales, is the original Velcro, and loves to stick to-gether. Add moisture and heat to wool, then agitate, and you've permanently velcroed wool into felt. The Romans discovered this when they put sheepskin, fleece side down, under their saddles. Horse sweat, the heat of its body, and the motion of the rider felted the fleece.

These mittens really open my eyes to the idea that not only is wool great for clothing and other uses, it's also great for reusing. And since my recycling skills have slipped a bit, reusing is something I should consider.

Most Americans aren't great at reusing clothing. We basically do three things with our clothes: We buy them. We wash them. We throw them away.

According to a report on the environmental impacts of clothing called "Waste Couture," globalization has made it possible for clothing companies to move their factories to low-labor-cost countries and produce clothing at prices so low consumers consider the clothing almost disposable. It's fast fashion, the equivalent of fast food. China has emerged as the world's leader in fast fashion, accounting for 30 percent of all clothing exports. Each year, Americans purchase approximately 1 billion garments made in China. We're not buying clothes to last, we're buying them to make ourselves feel good. Short-term fun.

What effect does cheap clothing have on consumers? Says Ellen Ruppel Shell, author of *Cheap: The High Cost of Discount Culture*, "Cheap objects resist involvement. We tend to invest less in their purchase, care, and maintenance, and that's part of what makes them so attractive."

Apparently we *like* that our clothing doesn't last because then we get to buy more. Perhaps that's why wool clothing has fallen out of favor, except with business suits. Wool clothing holds up too well and lasts too long, darn it. How can I justify buying that funky new sweater if my wool sweaters still look great?

Once we've bought the clothing, we wash it to excess. Someone studied all the energy consumed in the life of a cotton T-shirt and concluded that 60 percent of the energy was burned *after* the consumer bought the T-shirt through washing and drying the shirt twenty-five times. Because cotton readily absorbs sweat and body odor, it gets a bit rank without regular washing. Because wool *doesn't* absorb odors, it just needs to be hung out in the fresh air for a few hours, brushed a bit, and then worn again.

Synthetic fabrics take less energy to clean because they dry so quickly, which might be the best thing—the only positive thing—one can say about the environmental impacts of synthetic fibers. And here's another idea—drying all those things on a clothesline takes the least amount of energy. At least that's one energy-saving activity I do regularly.

So when we're done with our fast fashions, what next? Melissa and I keep a big black plastic bag in our closet that we fill periodically and take to a thrift shop that gleans clothing to sell in their shop, then ships the rest to developing countries.

According to the EPA Office of Solid Waste, Americans throw away more than sixty-eight pounds of clothing per person, per year. This figure is rapidly growing as clothing becomes even cheaper, and fashions change even faster. About ten pounds of this gets recycled or reused, leaving over fifty-eight pounds per person per year going straight to the dump. If a piece of clothing sent to the landfill is made of a natural fiber like cotton, silk, or wool, that clothing will eventually become one with the earth. True, it doesn't happen overnight, but it does happen. Synthetic fabrics are light and soft and we all wear the stuff. But when I buy a piece of synthetic clothing, I rarely consider that because it's plastic, it's going to be taking up space on the planet for *quite* some time. Petroleum-derived products are designed *not* to biodegrade, so they survive for decades in landfills.

So now I'm going to pay more attention to those old wool sweaters. Crispina ffrench (yes, dear reader, this is correct—two f's, no cap; do not send corrections to my editor) wrote a book called *The Sweater Chop Shop*, showing how to felt old wool sweaters, take them apart, then piece together new sweaters, scarves, and pillows. As her book says, "Recycle, Re-create, Re-enjoy."

In *Knit Green*, Joanne Seiff echoes the idea that there's lots of room for us to be environmentally creative. She writes that "it's fashionable right now to buy our way toward sustainability," and that consumers are attracted by advertising to buy new environmentally responsible products. As an alternative, she presents lots of ways knitters can reduce, reuse, and recycle.

My favorite wool sweater—a thick burgundy crew neck—kept me toasty for ten years. (It kept Melissa warm before that, but I stole it from her.) Then the neckline ripped a bit, and it became my "chore" sweater for the next ten years, until now the neckline has almost totally separated from the body of the sweater. The sleeves look as if an alien has burst out of each elbow. A knitting friend looks it over, shaking her head sadly. Even the most expert patch job may not work.

But Crispina and Joanne's books have opened my eyes to the beauty of re-enjoying wool rather than throwing it away. I could unravel my burgundy sweater and knit up a few dog toys using a pattern in Joanne's book. Or I could felt the sweater and make pot holders for my sister. I like this idea of unvirgin wool.

Or is that nonvirgin wool?

Formerly virgin wool?

Wool with patina?

Whatever name we choose, the sheep wore the wool for a year. Then I wore the sweater for twenty. My sister might use the pot holder for another ten.

Wool is the Energizer Bunny of the fiber world. No wonder it inspires so many fans.

We Are the Champions (of Sheep)

Sheep don't get a lot of press coverage; they are shyly in the background while horses, cattle, hogs, rabbits, and even llamas catch the eye of the public.

—RON PARKER, *THE SHEEP BOOK*

Although wool might be the star of the fiber world, I'm sad to say that sheep don't really stand up for themselves. They just quietly go about their lives, even as they continue to disappear from the planet.

How can this be happening? Perhaps because people consider sheep and wool boring. Sheep don't come with lots of flashy applications. They don't have any USB ports for flash drives. (Please note: Sheep don't have ports for *anything*. Remember, we want to love sheep in a healthy and platonic and non-gross sort of way.)

Technology ignores sheep. Does Wii make a sheep-shearing game? Nope. Now *there* would be some exercise. To inject a note of reality, you could wrestle your dog (or your spouse or child) to the ground and hold him there while you practice your shearing.

Sheep are just steady, reliable, unchanging. Today's sheep is much like the sheep of 10,000 years ago. They do an excellent job of being exactly what they are, something that can't be said for many humans, including myself.

Sheep are placid, naughty, stubborn, and protective, but sheep are not what nearly everyone thinks they are: stupid. So I willingly take on the role of Sheep's Champion.

I meet a delightful older woman at a birthday party, and when she learns I raise sheep, she leans closer, as if we're about to share a private joke.

"Sheep are so dumb, aren't they!"

The first 100 times this happened to me, I smiled politely, a little stunned that people would tell me I'm devoting my life to stupid animals. The second 100 times I grew a spine and shook my head, saying, "No, not really," then let it drop.

But now I challenge Hells Angels and stand up for myself. I'm cranky. I'm "ornery," as Dad calls it, and it's only a matter of time before I erupt in a public and not-so-appropriate way. When this poor woman played the "stupid" card, I was done being the sweet, patient shepherd.

"No, sheep are not dumb," I blast back. "They are sheep. Their three main goals are to eat, stay safe, and protect their young. That's it."

Cattle farmers and ranchers expect sheep to act like cattle, so when they don't, a sheep is suddenly stupid. This wrongheaded idea came from our history. Range wars heated up as the American

West was settled, and cattle ranchers hated sharing the grazing land with sheep. They called sheep "woolly maggots" and told everyone who'd listen how stupid sheep were. They left poison out on the open range for the sheep to eat, unfortunately poisoning their own cattle now and then. Cattlemen shot entire flocks dead, and they shot the sheepherders as well. The idea that sheep should act just like cattle is ridiculous. A sheep is one-tenth the size of a steer or cow and has reason to be more skittish.

I press on, even though I can tell the woman would rather be going over Niagara Falls in a barrel than hearing the rest of The Speech.

"Sheep understand food. They understand danger. They understand caring for their babies. We humans should be so focused. If you understand the sheep's motives, and understand their flight zones, sheep are easy."

The woman checks her watch, shoots desperate glances at her husband, then finally excuses herself, muttering she's due for a colonoscopy and now seems as good a time as any.

But I'm not done. Sheep aren't born with an understanding of gates or tractors or the knowledge that if they don't get themselves into the barn *right now* the farmer will miss the kickoff for the Super Bowl.

Sheep have two flight zones, shaped like cones, that serve as brilliant protection. One cone spreads backward from its head. If you approach a sheep directly from behind or from slightly to the side, you'll step into this flight zone and the sheep will surge forward like a thoroughbred coming out of the gate at the Kentucky Derby. Melissa and I, and our border collie, have found it handy that sheep have this personal bubble.

The sheep has a second flight zone, this cone reaching from its head forward. If you approach a sheep from the front and step inside this zone, will the sheep turn around and run in the opposite direction?

No, she will not. This is the downright clever part. That sheep is going to do the last thing you'd expect. If you step into that forward flight zone, the ewe will shoot straight *toward* you, a white blurred streak that passes within inches of your useless hands, leaving you standing there, mouth agape. You will both look and feel stupid. You will understand that even though you have more brain cells than a sheep, you have the reaction time of a slug.

On our farm, moving sheep from one spot to another is a delicate dance between sheep and shepherd. It's stepping slowly in and out of the correct flight zone, gently nudging the flock in the desired direction. But you only have one or two tries at moving the sheep through that gate or into that barn. If you're clumsy or in a hurry and the sheep miss the gate or the barn, good luck. It's going to be halftime before you make it back inside.

Why? Because the sheep know. They know you're going to give them shots if they go through that gate. They know you're going to shear them naked if they go into the barn. As you flail your arms and pant and sweat and forget all about flight zones, the look on those woolly faces is clear: "What do you think we are—stupid?"

Regrettably, I don't really deliver the above lecture to the woman at the birthday party. Instead, my crankiness erupts on the drive home and Melissa has to sit through it. Talk about preaching to the choir. But next time, I resolve not to hold back. I'll deliver that lecture. And then I'll use the line our friend Lori lets slip now and then: "Oh, did I say that out loud?"

As humans, some of us try to avoid being racist, or sexist, or ageist. I think we should also avoid judging animal species as well. As every culture and gender and age has its own merits, so does every animal. Sheep are exactly what they should be: sheep.

Of course, being a champion of sheep doesn't require that one own sheep. This means millions could pick up the cause, even if the nearest sheep is hundreds of miles away.

It also means that I, too, could love sheep without actually owning any.

I'd Turn Back
If I Were You

I was wrong to grow older. Pity. I was so happy
as a child.

—Antoine de Saint-Exupéry

I read self-help books now and then, even though I dislike their
format, their tone, and the insane income their authors make. Yet
invariably I pick up one tiny gem in each self-help book I read. My
latest is a book that characterizes my emotions as an elephant, a
big animal that goes where it wants, does what it wants. These last
few years, my elephant has been running roughshod over poor
Melissa, but she sticks to the relationship as tightly as wool fibers
stick to each other.

According to the book, my rational side is a wee little rider
perched atop the elephant. The rider spends a great deal of energy

trying to move the elephant in the right direction, to keep her under control. My rider is exhausted and has thrown down the reins in disgust. My rider has given up, unable to figure out why she's stuck with such an unreasonable elephant. I imagine Melissa has had similar thoughts.

And then it happens. One day I'm so hot I can't breathe. I yank off my sweater (wool), and in a few minutes I return to normal. Wow. Was that what I thought it was? Then it happens again a few months later.

Wow *again*. Am I really of that age? Could this be why my elephant has overpowered my rider? All doubt flees when my hormones begin doing the Riverdance stomp on my body. It's mildly amusing when I have one flash every two months, but then the next fall I start having hot flashes every forty minutes, all day long, and each flash feels as if I'm being suffocated under a pile of steaming blankets (wool). I stand outside in my underwear (not wool, not yet) trying to cool off.

Every generation that has come before me, including my mother and my grandmothers, went through this transition quietly and discreetly with nary a public complaint. I've read enough to know that menopause isn't an illness but a natural progression to the next stage of life, one that women are supposed to embrace as they move gracefully from "mother" to "wise crone."

Graceful, my ass. Wise crone, my now-larger ass.

There's nothing more tedious than a middle-aged woman who thinks she's the first to experience hormonal fluctuations. But as the typical baby boomer, I don't do discreet. I do "Why *me?*" Not only do we boomers grumble, stunned this is happening, but we need to tell everyone *all* about it. We're possibly the first generation to grow old without actually maturing.

Everything related to my body is changing, and I don't like it. What happened to the hair on my forearms? One day here, the next day gone, as if reabsorbed by my body. My biggest fear is that the hair will one day reemerge out my ears. I'll look like my sheep.

When the hot flashes worsen, it takes all my strength not to dissolve into an imitation of the Wicked Witch of the West, moaning, "I'm melting. I'm melting. . . ." I perfect my Insomnia Act, going week upon week without sleep. My irritability and impatience reach epic proportions, but I decide to ignore them. If I don't give menopause any attention, maybe it will go away.

This mature approach ends the day I stand staring at the knife beside the kitchen sink, thinking that if I stick the knife into my arm, maybe all this will end.

Okay. Crying over Elvis is one thing, but this is crazy talk.

I dash to the doctor and plead for hormones, even though I'd vowed never to take them. I return home with both hormones and sleeping pills. They work, but as a result, all the free-ranging calories in the atmosphere attach themselves to my body like metal filings onto a magnet. My jeans have now permanently shrunk.

Things get wonky. When Melissa snaps at me, I snap back, but some days I cleverly take the initiative and snap first. My previously gentle nagging switches to imperious commands. And Melissa has begun exhibiting her own signs—irritability, sudden mood swings. She'll be happy one minute, then terribly sad the next, unable to sort any of it out. If one menopausal woman in the house is trouble, two is a spectacularly bad idea. We should post a sign at the entrance to our driveway: "I'd turn back if I were you."

So. Now I know. My discontent, my crankiness, my wanting to flee the farm and move into an RV, all of that might just be the result of the hormonal wackiness that comes to those in middle age.

It's why I cuss out guys peeing in the ditch, why I flash my middle finger at speeding motorcyclists. If a company could bottle the anger of menopausal baby boomers, our country could replace fossil fuel as its main source of energy. My body is aging without my permission, so I'm resentful and immature and pissed off.

To help tame my menopausal beast, perhaps I need to find some way to connect with the farm on my own terms, some way to make it not only Melissa's dream but my own. I'm standing in the middle of my life, in the middle of a solid relationship, in the middle of the country, in the middle of a flock of sheep. There are worse places to be.

Oh, the irony of it all, for this is when the Goddess of Hardworking Shepherds reaches down from the heavens with her powerful little wand and taps us on our heads—tap, tap, tap. Apparently she is bored with middles. She wants to see what the end looks like.

Earlier I wrote that to be truly sheepish, one needs a shepherd, sheep, a shearer, a market for the sheep products, and lambs. There's one more thing required: a sense of humor.

The only way Melissa and I have survived to the middle of this farm, and this relationship, is by laughing—at the sheep, the llamas, the goats, the chickens, and at ourselves. This is good, because given what happens next, laughing is about all we can do.

PART

FOUR

Unravel

Something's Up

The farmer has to be an optimist or he wouldn't
still be a farmer.

—WILL ROGERS

On most livestock farms, the animals must reproduce because the
farmer is in the business of making more of them. For thousands
of years we shepherds have been controlling the breeding of our
animals, trying to create the finest wool or the tenderest meat.
Farmers still do this today; the only difference is that on many
farms the male and female never meet.

This virtual speed mating is called artificial insemination. Basically, you have an expensive ram with great genes and a healthy li-
bido. Instead of dragging him all over the planet to visit the ladies,
the farmer gives the ram a plastic cup and two back issues of *Totally
Shorn Ewes*, and soon there's some sperm available. Farmers buy the
sperm, a vet inserts it, the ewe walks away, and biology takes over.

195

We, however, run an old-fashioned farm. Because we let the ram and ewe actually meet and actually mate, sheep sex is an exciting event that begins December 17.

As we once again approach this date, we solve the problem of Melissa's low energy. She's been anemic for months. No wonder she's been dragging around the farm. She undergoes a laparoscopic hysterectomy in the fall and as she recovers, the Backup Farmer sproings into action.

The doctor assures us Melissa will be back to her old self in a month. It takes longer than that. For Melissa, recuperation means sneaking out of the house to move things around in the barn until I figure out she's escaped and am forced to use my Angry Voice to march her back into the house. This happens day after day. I consider handcuffing her to the dining room table. December drags on.

Soon, it's time. We let the tension build because it helps the ewes start cycling together. To do this, we put our ram Erik on one side of the electric fence and a group of hot-to-trot ewes on the other. We let them pace back and forth along those 5,000 volts for a few weeks until the sexual tension snaps louder than the fence. Then we strap a harness across Erik's chest that holds a big flat green crayon. Every time he mounts and successfully breeds a ewe, he'll leave a telltale green mark on her back.

On December 17 we open the gate and Erik rushes toward the ewes. Because a ewe is ready and willing to breed only about every seventeen days, Erik must find those ewes in that part of their cycle today. He sniffs backside after backside, curling his upper lip delicately to better inhale the ewes' scents. Finally he finds one. She stands still, batting her eyelashes. He mounts. Boom-boom-boom. It's over. The green marker does its job. On this farm, instead of the Scarlet Letter, we have the Viridian Smudge.

Now that there's been ovine love, there will be babies in five months, in mid-May, and we'll spin through the cycle of our year again. But as I feed and water the animals every day, I make note of the green smudges. Hmmm. There aren't many. I stand around watching, huddled against the barn wall to get out of the wind that's lowering the 20°F temperature down to zero. I massage my face so it doesn't freeze into a confused scowl. It may sound kinky that I watch our sheep breed, but if something goes wrong with the breeding, something goes wrong with the farm.

My suspicions grow. Other than his first day on the "job," Erik isn't getting much "action." Is he sick? Is he injured? Low on energy? Holding out for some long-legged Swedish ewes?

Something's up, but it's clearly not the ram.

Adventures of the
Backup Farmer

'Tis but a flesh wound.
—*MONTY PYTHON AND THE HOLY GRAIL*

I tell Melissa that if she doesn't stop sneaking out of the house to work in the shed, all the internal organs still left inside her will come undone and head for the nearest exit. This finally convinces her to stay put, so I can go about winter chores without worrying.

Luckily everything is closer during the winter. As E. B. White wrote,

I forgot that sheep come up in late fall and join the family circle. At first they visit the barn rather cautiously, eat some hay, and depart. But after one or two driving storms they abandon the pasture altogether, draw up chairs around the fire, and settle down for the winter. They become as much a part of your group as your dog, or your Aunt Maudie.

We, too, move our sheep in closer for winter. They have lots of hay, and access to the barn in an ice storm or heavy snowstorm. Everyone hunkers down. But the animals still require water and checking every day. Doing chores involves suiting up in my insulated Carhartt overalls, insulated Carhartt barn coat, ugly red hat with the ear flaps, and big chopper mittens. I head for the big barn where forty ram lambs are eating lots of hay and small amounts of corn until they reach market weight. If I were to show you a photo of some of these ram lambs, you'd think two things: one, that they were larger than you expected, and two, that they looked sweet and innocent. Hardly. Ram lambs can be naughty boys.

As usual, we put those green feeder panels around the hay bales—one bale at a time, not four. Once the animals have eaten all the hay they can reach, Melissa or I "stir" the hay, moving it from the center so the lambs can more easily reach it. Although we're tough enough not to name our sheep, coddling them is apparently acceptable.

Most shepherds castrate their young ram lambs, but we don't. Male lambs grow faster with all their boy parts intact. As a result, our ram lambs are feisty. They like to slam their rock-hard heads together for fun.

"Stirring" hay requires that I turn my back on the lambs and lean over the panel with a pitchfork. I'm wearing my thick insulated bib overalls, which, alarmingly, have shrunk just as much as my jeans. When I bend over the feeder panel to stir the hay, I present a tempting target. After a few weeks of this, there comes the day when one joker in the bunch can't resist. While my back is

turned, the ram—possibly egged on by the rest of the lambs—
lowers his head and rams me.

Whoa! My hips slam against the feeder panel, the rest of me
pitches forward into the hay. I struggle up, sputtering, spitting out
hay, and whirl to face the culprit. He's gone. He's melted back into
the group, and every single one of them looks at me in total inno-
cence. "It wasn't me," say forty pairs of eyes.

Grumbling, I turn back and resume working. That damn lamb
does it again. I right myself faster this time, then whirl around. By
now some of the lambs can't repress their snickers, and a few
others look worried, knowing they'll all be punished for the hijinks
of one rowdy guy.

They're right. I deliver a scathing lecture on the wisdom of
ramming the person who's making sure they have plenty to eat,
and soon even the toughest of the lambs is shuffling his hooves,
unable to look me in the eye.

I move to the other side of the hay bale and finish my job. But
when I leave the pen, I pass a small group of snickering lambs, and
I can smell trouble. Sure enough, one of them actually has the
nerve to say, directly to my face, "Nice target."

I report back to Melissa. We agree that male lambs are all
hoodlums, the lot of them.

Hanging out in another section of the winter pasture are the
ewes. Winter doesn't bother the ladies, but they do have one bad
habit. As they eat hay from the feeders, they pull it out and drop
it. They walk around with it in their mouths and drop it. Soon
there's an island of hay in the snow. The hay is totally wasted;
once they've peed on it, they don't want to eat it. Then it snows
on top of this dropped hay. Then more hay goes down. Then more
snow.

Some people think that sheep need access to a barn all year long, that it's cruel to keep them outside. Please. These girls are carrying their own barns on their backs, about eight pounds of the stuff. The sheep use the barn during ice storms, since these can be nasty, and after they've been sheared late March, but that's it.

Our girls are content to hang out in the snow. And when they lie down at night to sleep, an amazing sight appears the next morning. The snowy pasture is dotted with small ovals of hay, which totally mystifies the Backup Farmer until she works it through. The sheep are so warm that the heat from their body melts through the snow, revealing hay from the layer below.

Melissa feels guilty that I must do chores. She begins feeling better now that she's figured out what "rest and recuperation" actually means, but I don't want her to take over the chores too soon. However, I am getting tired, since negotiating the farm in winter can be hard with all the ice and snow. Then comes the day I step back too quickly and slip on a chunk of frozen soil. Like in a cartoon, both my legs fly straight out, my body hovers in the air until my left buttock is centered directly over the frozen mound, then I slam to the ground.

Fairly positive I've broken my bumfitt, I lie there quietly, thinking about Elvis.

And thinking about how, in my life as Backup Farmer, one part of my anatomy seems to be getting more than its share of bruises. And thinking about how being rammed in the butt certainly distinguishes my life from most other lives.

After ten minutes I collect myself, walk back to the house, and find Melissa. "Okay, you can start doing chores now," I say.

Holy Hanky Panky, Batman

The conception of two people living together
for twenty-five years without having a cross
word suggests a lack of spirit only to be ad-
mired in sheep.

—ALAN PATRICK HERBERT

Melissa takes over chores midwinter and I dive back into my writing. The lambs are now market weight, so we hire our friend Paul to trailer them to the processing plant. Customers begin visiting the farm to pick up their meat orders. Farm tours in January are short. I stand by the house and point up toward the sheep barn: "The ewes are up there. The steers are over there. Let's go inside for hot chocolate and cookies."

All is as it should be. Then one early February morning Melissa notices a ewe with a round, tight udder, full of milk. *What?* The udder only fills up when the sheep is days away from giving birth, not months away as these sheep should be.

According to our schedule, Erik did his thing in December, so lambs will be born in mid-May. Yet if this ewe is about to give birth in February, she'd done the deed three months too early, sometime in September, when we were busy figuring out Melissa's anemia.

The next day we put the flock into the handling facility, moving each ewe into the chute so Melissa can reach between the ewe's back legs, through the long wool, and feel the udder. The first one has a full udder. The second one has a full udder. So does the third. This isn't an isolated incident of one ewe getting pregnant. One of those rambunctious ram lambs, back in September, had hopped a few fences and been very, very busy. Our only consolation, of course, is that the ram lamb was now in someone's freezer.

It turns out that over two-thirds of the flock, or twenty-five sheep, have udders that are either very full, or on their way to being so. Now we understand. Back in December, Erik wasn't breeding the ewes because most of them were All. Ready. Pregnant.

Let's say that phrase together, and make sure you grit your teeth to get the full emotional experience: The sheep were All. Ready. Pregnant.

Why should we be surprised? After all, ten years earlier we'd had a similar problem with a randy ram lamb. Yet we never waver in our belief that we, the shepherds, are in control. But in our previous bout with unauthorized sheep sex, the lambs had come in mid-March. In Minnesota, early February is an entirely different climate than mid-March.

Exhausted, we resolve to get through yet another crisis. We are Super Shepherds: strong, independent women who can do anything. We'll find some way to enclose our open-sided barn. We'll buy two dozen heat lamps. Melissa will get up twice a night to warm any lambs born in the cold. But because she still hasn't recovered her spark since surgery, buckling down and pushing through feels wrong to me.

Sometimes the best path is also the hardest. The next morning, while Melissa is showering, I call Paul and Lela, leaving a message on their machine. Do they know anyone interested in buying twenty-five ewes on the verge of giving birth? Then I call Drew with the same question. He comes up with a few people and says he'll ask them. I call Joe and Bonnie with the same plea. They, too, put their heads together and come up with a few names. I'm touched at how quickly our friends "get" what I'm trying to do.

Paul calls me back, and I tell him the whole story. When we're done complaining about sheep and their lawless ways, Paul chuckles and gets down to business. "Say, Cath, I know you won't believe this, but last week Lela and I were talking about finding some sheep to lamb out this winter."

My heart leaps. "You're kidding."

I can hear the smile in his voice, and see him shaking his head, as amazed as I am. "Nope, I'm not. How 'bout if we come over this weekend and look 'em over?"

"Excellent."

When Melissa joins me in the living room, squeaky clean and ready to face the day's battles, I tell her what I've done. "We need to sell the pregnant sheep, and Paul and Lela would take good care of them."

"No, we're not selling them," Melissa says.

"Yes, we are," I say.

"No."

"Why not?"

Melissa hesitates. "Because this is a farm. It's what I do. Selling them would. . . . What would I do then?"

I think about my idea to stop farming. This isn't how I'd imagined it happening. This isn't what I wanted. Our decision involves complicated concepts like self-definition and self-worth and life's purpose. We know these twenty-five sheep personally. But I live with Melissa. I know her energy level. I know about all the stresses pressing down on her that have nothing to do with the farm. Her mother's health, never good, is declining rapidly and the end may be near. "We need to sell the sheep."

"No, we don't."

"Yes, we do."

Even though we aren't amused (yet) by this disaster, I have to appreciate the sneakiness of the adolescent ram. A teenage boy knows if he sneaks into his girlfriend's bedroom, he'd better not be there in the morning when Mom comes in. It turns out teenage sheep have the same instincts. He hops a few fences, bangs many ladies, then knows enough to hop back where he belongs so he doesn't get caught.

See what I mean? Sheep *are* smart.

We've always found it amusing, or at least interesting, that all the men sheep producers we know castrate their rams, but we don't.

Ha. Those things are coming off from now on.

No more Ms. Nice Lesbians.

Dividing
Up the Cake

A compromise is the art of dividing the cake in
such a way that everyone believes he has the
biggest piece.

—LUDVIG ERHARD

Melissa and I wrangle for two days. She accuses me of always taking shortcuts to make my life easier. (Will I never live down that
recycling debacle?) I accuse her of being unrealistic about our ability to ensure newborn lambs will survive in February.

Melissa's solution is to make a list, so she writes down the
tag numbers of the twenty-five ewes and begins examining their
records to see what sort of mothers they are and how many
lambs they've had. I suppose this is one way to deal with stress,
but it isn't nearly as productive as standing in front of the open

refrigerator door and eating anything not stuck to the cold shelves.

We can put off our final discussion no longer, since Paul and Lela are coming soon. It's a warm enough day, so we bundle up and walk out to the shed. Going to a neutral spot seems a smart thing to do. We sit down in the garage on hard logs waiting to be split, and despite the sun spilling through the open door, we hunch over against the cold.

Melissa shows me her list. Of the twenty-five pregnant ewes, there are five she absolutely will not give up. Their lambing records are too good. Or they're the offspring of some of our best ewes. She isn't willing to let these genetics walk off the farm. And there are four ewes with physical problems, like udders that don't work well any more, and we'd planned to cull them from the flock. Neither of us wants to sell a cull animal to friends.

I do the math. Out of twenty-five sheep, there are nine she won't sell. "So we could sell the other sixteen?"

The open garage door is horizontal above our heads. The three pigeons living in our shed scrabble overhead, their tiny claws scratching harshly on the metal door. In the mood I'm in, it feels just like nails on a chalkboard. I jam my hands deeper into my recycled wool sweater mittens. "I know this is really hard for you. I get that. But I'm really worried about your health. I'm worried we won't be able to keep newborn lambs alive. May we sell those sixteen?" Other farmers lamb without heat in their barns, so I know it's possible, but I'd never met anyone who lambed in the dead of winter in a three-sided barn open to the elements.

Melissa looks me in the eye, checks her list again, then leaps across the abyss. She nods, her cheeks red from the cold. We can sell sixteen of the sheep.

I breathe easier. We might just work this out. Yet while I appreciate the sacrifice she's making, we still have nine sheep giving birth in an open, unheated barn. Melissa's health and stress issues aren't going away whether we lamb twenty-five or nine.

My blood turns to molten iron, then hardens into steel. "We have to sell them all."

If Melissa and I tighten our jaws any harder, we'll crack teeth.

"I won't sell culls to a friend," she says, and I agree. Culls these sheep might be, but they're still our responsibility and we aren't going to close our eyes and ship off the problem.

But then inspiration bends down and whispers the solution in my ear. It seems so obvious. "We'll explain to Paul and Lela that these are cull sheep. We'll charge less for those four ewes. They'll get lambs from them, then they can sell the ewes." Melissa and I look at each other with sudden hope. Excellent idea. We've solved what to do with twenty of the sheep. White Girl is in the batch of pregnant ewes to be culled. We will sell her to Paul, then he'll decide what to do with her.

We have five pregnant sheep left on the list. One of them is Black Girl. Melissa bends over her clipboard, as if protecting the five animals.

"That leaves the five you think are too good too sell," I say. "How can they be so special?"

More jaw tightening. "They are." For five minutes she passionately outlines the history and personality of each one. Then she suddenly straightens. "What if we don't sell the ewes, but instead *loan* them to Paul and Lela? They get the lambs and we get the five ewes back when the lambs are old enough to be weaned."

The tension blows away like a puff of smoke and we actually grin at each other. Even though creativity often shows up late for my parties, it does eventually arrive. I resolve to remember this the next time I'm sitting in front of a blank computer screen, cursing J. K. Rowling because she's stolen my muse.

Paul and Lela love the look of our sheep, so we negotiate a price, then Paul picks up the ewes on a Monday afternoon, five days after Melissa saw the first udder. That night both Melissa and I are very quiet.

The first lamb is born the next morning on Paul and Lela's farm. Over the next two weeks, fifty-four lambs are born, including many sets of twins, and a few sets of triplets. White Girl has quadruplets. Melissa is proud of our "girls," but heartbroken at the same time.

She knows these sheep. She knows their faces, their personalities. These animals aren't just beasts with ear tag numbers. We've bred them for years, striving to keep the best traits and eliminate bad ones. She knows that No. 703 is No. 66's daughter. She knows this one had been born a triplet. She remembers delivering that ewe under the trees on a rainy May day.

A small piece of Melissa's soul follows our sheep to Paul and Lela's. A piece of mine does as well.

More Babies

Like sheep that get lost nibbling away at the
grass because they never look up, we often focus so much on ourselves and our problems
that we get lost.

—ALLEN KLEIN

The twenty-five very pregnant sheep are gone. We have seventeen sheep remaining that won't give birth for another three
months because they were all bred—hopefully—at the right time,
by Erik in December. In addition, we have a few other sheep. We
know No. 66 isn't pregnant because she's getting old and has
earned her retirement. Our pet sheep, No. 75/101, has had mastitis too many times, the illness that had killed her mother, so we've
decided she'll remain on the farm as a pet. Yikes. How did it come
to pass that the tough muffins are keeping both pet sheep and retired sheep?

After we sell the ewes to Paul and Lela, we follow through on
plans to visit friends in California. Unfortunately, when Melissa
felt each ewe's udder to determine which sheep were pregnant, she
missed four. We learn this a few days after we fly to California,
when the teenager doing chores is thrust into the world of winter
lambing without notice. Alex does an amazing job. When she finds
a set of twins in the snow, one dead, the other alive, she moves
both the live lamb and the mom into the barn. She does the same
with the next ewe a day later. In moving a third ewe, the ewe in-
jures its leg. We try to help Alex as much as we can, but we're
1,000 miles away. Those times she can't reach our cells, she calls
Amelia, the original Pasture Goddess. It fills Amelia with pride,
and a bit of awe, to find herself dispensing advice.

When we return home, the fourth ewe gives birth. Time to
take stock. We have two healthy lambs. We have two baby lambs
in a laundry basket in the house, one who's been unable to stand
since birth. We have an injured ewe with a lamb that isn't getting
enough to eat.

The good news is the little lamb that can't stand grows stronger
every day. In a few days, he can get to his feet unassisted, then he
begins staggering around. But since there isn't room in a laundry
basket for him to get the hang of walking, I build a pen in the unheated barn, complete with a thick bed of straw, a towel-wrapped
heating pad tucked inside a cavelike box, and a heat lamp. Then I
cover the pen with enough wood to retain heat but allow the lambs
to see out the sides and watch the steers. The 600-pound steers are
fascinated with the six-pound lambs and stare and stare. Soon the
lamb is walking without stumbling, and eating like a horse.

The ewe with the broken leg isn't doing well. She's in a great
deal of pain, then develops pneumonia; the leg is infected. On top

of that, the ewe is wild with fear, now associating any human with pain. Melissa continues to treat her, and to supplement her lamb with a bottle, but we're both concerned. Melissa often works hard to save an animal's life, treating it for weeks, only to be forced to accept defeat and put the animal down, but she's determined to help this ewe get better.

Late one evening, Melissa calls me from the barn. She's spent thirty minutes on the phone with our vet discussing the ewe's condition, and it's not good. Melissa has a choice—watching the ewe suffer every day, in so much pain despite painkillers that she can barely walk five feet to the water bucket—or end her suffering.

Over the phone, she tells me where to find the handgun, and which bullets to bring. It's cold and dark as I walk up to the barn, so familiar with our land I don't need a flashlight. The barn is cold, but well lit. In the far pen the two healthy lambs and their moms nibble on hay. The injured ewe is sitting back in a sheep "chair," basically a hammock designed to sit a sheep upright so Melissa can trim hooves or treat injuries.

Melissa and I talk quietly for a few minutes, concerned about how Alex will take the news, worried she'll feel responsible since the injury happened on her watch. But sheep hurt themselves, they hurt each other, they hurt farmers, and farmers accidentally hurt them now and then. It happens.

Melissa catches the injured ewe's lamb and hands her to me. The ewe bleats for her baby, so I hold the lamb near her face, trying not to cry as the ewe nuzzles the lamb. Then I tuck the lamb inside my coat and trudge back to the little barn where the other two bottle lambs live. I put her in the pen with the twins, then go into the house to prepare a bottle so she can fall asleep with a full stomach.

Having an animal sick or in pain is something that never leaves you during the day, since a tiny part of your brain is always worrying about it. I don't hear the shot, but later Melissa says it only took one. I put an ad in the paper for bottle lambs, and in a few days a nice young woman buys all three.

And thus ends our winter lambing.

Not Exactly a Goddess

Laugh at yourself first, before anyone else can.

—Elsa Maxwell

Spring comes. There are thirteen pregnant ewes, three ewes with lambs, and a handful of retired pets. With only thirteen pregnant ewes, I don't worry about lining up all the Pasture Goddesses. Mary H. comes for a week, but only two sheep give birth while she's here. "So," Melissa says after Mary leaves. "Who'll help me out in the pasture now?"

Amelia is working full time. Bonnie won't be done teaching for another two weeks. "Lucky girl," I say, "you get me."

During a normal lambing season, Melissa might help at *most* six ewes out of fifty give birth. At most six lambs out of 100 born might die. So if you're only lambing out thirteen ewes, wouldn't it make sense to expect that the numbers of difficult births and dead lambs would both be down?

214

Yes, it would, but since this is the year the Goddess of Shepherds has frowned upon us, it's also the year that four out of thirteen ewes need help. We lose five lambs out of twenty-nine born. We have nearly the same number of problems with thirteen sheep that we have with fifty. It's a grueling week.

One morning finds Melissa and me on our knees in the dewy pasture, me holding the reclining ewe by her head and Melissa at the other end helping with a difficult labor. Both lambs are stillborn. That night we're on another spot in the same pasture, in the same position. Both lambs are stillborn. An immensely painful day.

Another day we stand in the pasture, the sun beating down on our heads, as we puzzle over a family mess. Two ewes both want all three lambs and the lambs don't know which mother is theirs. We finally decide one lamb is a single and belongs to the younger ewe, who's never given birth before. Melissa puts temporary fences around each group so the ewes won't keep stealing each other's lambs.

The next day the same thing happens with two more new mothers, only there are four lambs. Holy smokes. I'm so impatient I nearly jump up and down. What's wrong with these sheep? At this point I wish I were playing Farmville so I could just log off.

Melissa is used to these sorts of messes and begins searching for placentas. Since she picks them up every day, the only placentas on the ground this morning would be from the four lambs. Eventually Detective Farmer finds a single placenta, very fresh, then not far away she finds three older, drier placentas. One ewe had a single, the other ewe triplets. By watching the lambs, we identify the youngest and eventually sort the two families out.

One ewe has a problem with her udder, so we bring her up to the barn in the Rubbermaid cart pulled behind the four-wheeler, her lambs tucked in around her. We must also do this for another ewe. Both ewes and their lambs are eventually fine, but it's very hard work.

Melissa finds a lamb with entropion, an eye disorder in which the eyelid is turned inward and causes pain and blindness. She puts little silver clips, which she calls "eye spangles," on the eyelid to pull it away from the eyeball. I hold the lamb, squeeze my eyes shut, and turn away. I can't say why I turn away, since my eyes are closed, but it helps. Once the eye spangles correct the problem, they'll fall off when they're no longer needed.

Finally, the last pregnant ewe goes into labor, and of course needs help. The ewe has chosen the only bare spot in the pasture, so I lie in the dirt, holding the ewe down by the shoulder, while Melissa delivers the first lamb. She plops the baby in front of the ewe's face, which is also in front of mine. "Big boy," she announces as I stare, aghast, at the seemingly lifeless form. Melissa barks an order for me to clean him off, then returns to the ewe's back end where she pulls the second lamb and plops it next to the first. I towel off both wet lambs. They're a bit stunned to no longer be tucked inside the womb, but they're strong and healthy.

Melissa slips her arm back inside the ewe one more to time to check for a third lamb. Meanwhile, between all the fluid, and the ewe instinctively eating birth stuff off the lambs, and the pool of blood under the ewe's back end, I feel a little queasy. I rest my head on the ewe while Melissa finishes her job.

"It's remarkable how amazingly ill suited I am for this particular activity," I say.

Melissa smiles, which is nice to see. "This is not news to me."

Focus on Feet

One can never have enough socks.

—ALBUS DUMBLEDORE, HEADMASTER OF
HOGWARTS SCHOOL OF WITCHCRAFT AND WIZARDRY

To escape the harder parts of farming, I tentatively dip my toe deeper into the ocean of knitters and am immediately sucked in by a riptide. I find knitting groups, spinning clubs, craft councils, and a gazillion knitting blogs with creative names like Purls Before Swine, and InsubordiKnit. I join ravelry.com and lose entire days browsing through patterns and yarn.

Turns out knitting isn't just for the elderly anymore; it's for everyone, including men. The Craft Yarn Council of America estimates that the number of knitting men has increased in this century from 1.5 million to 2.6 million, making them about 5 percent of the knitting population. Many men and boys of the "skateboard" generation wanted to create their own hats, individualize their looks.

Male knitters aren't doing anything new. European sailors as far back as the fifteenth century knit their own sweaters, and knitting was popular in the United States for men during both World War I and World War II. And if men want to learn more about knitting, they don't have to read *Stitch and Bitch* by Debbie Stoller but can head straight for *Knitting with Balls*, by Michael del Vecchio.

I yearn to knit something more interesting than a scarf. The whole sweater thing is intimidating, and I don't wear hats and as yet have no relatives who need baby blankets. What's left? After lurking on blogs and Ravelry and talking with knitters, I realize the best item for me to tackle next is the sock, the one piece of clothing that seems ridiculous to make by hand because machines do them so well. Kathy knits socks because they're like miniature works of art in which she can refine her knitting and color-blending skills. Phyllis knits socks because they're easy to carry and don't take long. I begin, reluctantly, to explore the sock.

Wool has never been very great as a full leg stocking. Think thick. Think saggy and loose fitting. But wool stockings were manufactured by machine in England starting in 1599. Those machines were smuggled into other countries, and the Mennonites ended up in possession of a few. They brought them along when they emigrated to Pennsylvania in 1683, formed Germantown, and built the first woolen stocking factory in America.

Socks were used to barter with the Native Americans. A document in 1689 made mention of the Dutch trading six pairs of these stockings for one beaver skin. Heck of a deal. In 1676, Mary Rowlandson was captured by Indians in a Narragansett raid on her Lancaster, Massachusetts, home. She found it difficult to survive on the spare rations she was given, so when the Indians would raid more homes and bring back piles of picked-apart old stockings, she'd use the yarn to knit new stockings and barter them with the Indians for more food.

When Joseph Watt led a wagon train and a flock of sheep out west in 1848, it took them six months to travel from Missouri to Oregon. The winter was harsh, and many sheep died, but the hardy settlers took the fleece off the dead animals and knit 150 pairs of socks. During the Gold Rush that next spring, Watt traveled to California and sold the socks to the gold miners.

Although wool still doesn't make great pantyhose, it does make warm socks. Our friend Robin sends me a copy of her easy-to-follow sock pattern, which I study every afternoon over my glass of wine. Then I accompany Kathy to a St. Paul knitting store, where I'm exposed to the fascinating idea that commercial sock yarns are dyed by computer to create designs. All you have to do is sit down and knit with one of these skeins, and a colorful pattern emerges, with stripes or flowers or swirls. Magic.

There must be something to this sock craze, so I buy a skein of blue and purple variegated yarn. Socks are usually knit using four short needles. This is as awkward as it sounds. The needles are pointed at each end so you can knit from either end. Or if you're me, you can accidentally let your stitches slip off one needle while you're working with the others, thereby creating much sock-related cursing and confusion. I have so much trouble that I consider giving up. Why not buy socks from Wigwam Mills? It's going to take me ten to fifteen hours to knit this sock; a factory machine can spit one out every ninety seconds.

I struggle to get started and do it all wrong about three times. I finally resort to YouTube and get myself back on track, at least for a little while. I need help "turning" the heel. I need help with the gusset, the little triangle-shaped thingie near the heel that machine-knit socks don't seem to have. After help with these from Kathy, I march on solo to the toe and make a mess of it, but then I'm done. It looks like a sock for a deformed foot, but a sock nonetheless. I try another one, and only need help with the gusset. Even my toe turns out better.

I find knitting the sock to be more enjoyable than I'd expected. As I begin to get bored with the section I'm knitting, it's time to switch to the next part of the sock—the leg, the heel flap, the heel, the gusset, the foot, the toe.

Melissa likes the sock I knit for myself, so I measure her foot. Because she's not a fan of bright turquoise or pink, I choose a nice brown and green tweed for her sock. For the first time I success-fully make my way through the gusset on my own, partly on faith, partly by sticking the needle in different places until something works.

I proudly present Melissa with her very own homemade sock, knit with love and a bit of bravery.

"Very cool, "she says. "Where's the other one?"

The *other* one? Ungrateful wench.

Apparently if you don't have a farmer standing there demand-ing a second sock, many knitters find it boring to knit the same thing twice and never get around to making the second sock. I avoid the dreaded SSS (single sock syndrome) by promptly knit-ting a second sock.

I continue knitting socks. I love how they feel on my feet. Melissa loves how they feel on hers. And we anxiously await our yarn from Montana, hoping it will be suitable for me to knit into a sock, or perhaps two.

My Head Is
Full of Colors

Why do two colors, put one next to the other,
sing? Can one really explain this? No.

—PABLO PICASSO

Our yarn from Montana finally arrives on the UPS truck. To my inexperienced eyes, it looks like ordinary white yarn. I give Kathy a skein to try, and she says blushingly wonderful things about it. I think she's just being sweet. "Lovely! Great for cables! I want more!"

Nice to hear, but she's a dear friend and would of course say the yarn is great. Then while at a rally for health care reform, Kathy sits next to a friend of hers, a well-known designer of knit clothing and patterns. Annie teaches knitting all over the country, writes knitting books, designs patterns for *Vogue Knitting*, blogs, and raises two kids. Thinking about her life makes me beyond tired. But she watches Kathy knit and has to know where the yarn came from.

Annie isn't one to waste any time, so in less than a week she brings her family to the farm so she can meet us and meet our yarn. "So white. So soft," she says, stretching a bunch between her hands. "Great spring." Before I know it she has draped a skein over her knees and is winding it into a ball. She takes the yarn home and begins knitting, soon sending off an enthusiastic e-mail: "The more I work with your creamy, worsted weight yarn, the more I love it!"

We don't have any of the fancier fine wool breeds I see in fiber magazines, like Cormo, Merino, Romney, Rambouillet, or Blue-faced Leicester, but our yarn is still pronounced as lovely.

Melissa and I are intrigued. This fiber idea is fascinating, but I have no idea what to do next. Should we change our breeding? Should we sell through a Web site? Visit some of the over 100 fiber fairs held across the country every year?

I need a wool coach, so I ask Annie for help. She puts out the word on her widely read blog and the perfect coach responds. Joanne knits and spins and dyes and writes and knows sheep. She pronounces our roving as crisp and easy to spin. Apparently crisp-feeling wools are longer wearing and better for outer garments like a sweater or socks. The finer wools I'd been thinking of, like Merino, wouldn't stand up to the strain. I should have remembered that Thomas Jefferson had already discovered this.

Joanne likes the color, saying the natural wool is a bright white that has great potential both for selling as "natural white" and also for dyeing, because the yarn will dye a truer color than creamy or off-white yarn. To test it, Joanne dyes up a small batch using Black Cherry Kool-Aid. (Who knew one could do such a thing?) It turns out a lovely soft red.

I bombard her with questions about our sheep and dyeing and marketing and the meaning of life. She responds with wit and insight. Basically, we don't need to worry about introducing any of those fancier breeds into our flock because our fleece is just fine as it is. We might want to introduce a Corriedale ram to bring those wool qualities out even more. Melissa and I are amazed our fleece doesn't have to end up in carpeting. People might actually wear it.

Our brains spin with possibilities, but regardless of our future plans, the most immediate task is to dye the yarn we have. Dyeing seems a complex process, and my life is too full to make room for another project.

Annie suggests I contact a skilled dyer named London, who is happy to help. We meet at a coffeehouse halfway between our cities and I transfer bags and bags of white yarn to her car. When she asks what colors to dye the yarn, I'm so overwhelmed by the options I can't decide. Do what you think looks best, I say, and I drive home dreaming about color. My head is *full* of colors.

An Intimate Secret

The game of life is a game of boomerangs. Our
thoughts, deeds and words return to us sooner
or later with astounding accuracy.

—FLORENCE SCOVEL SHINN

There are few topics as intimate as underwear. I continue my
search for wool underwear and finally hit pay dirt. According to
The Shepherd magazine, a company called KentWool announced
a new technology that creates yarns "softer, more subtle, more
durable, and more functional" than any previous wool yarn. The
company proclaims that this product will turn wool from a two-
season product—fall and winter—into an all-season product.

This is a great idea. I contact Ramblers Way Farms, the Maine
clothing company developing products from this fabric. And their
product line is—get this!—*underwear*: undershirts, camisoles, boxers,
underpants, long johns and janes. The yarn is spun from superfine

fleece sheared from Rambouillet sheep raised in the United States. Innovation can happen with wool, and it can happen naturally by selectively breeding sheep for the desired fiber. The company was started by Tom and Kate Chappell, the couple who brought us Tom's of Maine toothpaste. Why get into wool underwear? As Tom explained in *Sheep Industry News*, "Because the older you get, the colder you get."

I like the philosophy of the company. The farm is powered by geothermal and solar energy. The wool is washed in a chlorine-free process. The packaging is made from recycled materials. Their trucks and tractors run on biofuels.

I order a pair of underwear. The price is ridiculously high, but I want to know if it's possible to make comfortable underwear out of wool.

Meanwhile, in our never-ending search to find relief for Melissa's headaches, we try an orthopedic surgeon. An MRI reveals she has the neck of a much older person, with blown discs and arthritic vertebrae. He proposes relieving Melissa's headaches by fusing several vertebrae. Here we are, facing another fall surgery. I will once again be Backup Farmer, as well as facing the deadlines of two writing contracts and caring for Melissa. Her recovery from this surgery will be much longer than from the hysterectomy.

The farm suddenly feels very large to both of us. The steers are at their market weight, so Melissa takes them to the processor. We're sad to see them go but excited about getting more calves in the spring after Melissa has recovered. That I must feed and care for seventeen sheep and three llamas feels complex. What if an animal gets sick? Treating a sick animal isn't one of my skills and having a vet come out will be expensive. So on the cusp of this early winter surgery of Melissa's, I'm faced with doing all of the farming tasks—feeding grain, feeding hay, moving panels to fresh bales in the snow, battling ice and frozen water hydrants, taking care of the chickens, cats, and dogs, getting the driveway plowed, feeding us, running all the errands, paying bills, taking care of Melissa, and writing two books due early the next spring. Even though I'm more hormonally balanced now, I have my limits, and the above list has just exceeded them. I regret that I'm not really Super Shepherd. No one's more disappointed in me than I am. We must sell all the sheep.

In early December, Melissa and I stand in the pasture looking at our animals. One sheep is the daughter of No. 39, a big, healthy sheep who'd been an excellent mother. Another ewe's cocoa brown fleece would make lovely yarn. There's No. 75/101, our big friendly bottle lamb. There's White Girl, who somehow ended up back here after lambing at Paul and Lela's; she has udder problems as well. Our dear old girl, No. 66, died quietly a month earlier.

We should sell all the sheep. Stop farming. Get real jobs. Take control of our lives again. But when we race up to that point of no return, both of us hesitate, even me. If we sell our sheep, we will never have this precise crossbreed again. Stepping over that line and selling all the sheep feels so final. We'd worked so hard to get this farm going, and yes, the last few years have been fraught with physical and family and financial and emotional troubles, but is letting go *really* what I want after fifteen years here?

We can walk away. We already have some off-farm income, so it's not as if we'll suddenly be out of money. We could rent the North Pasture to a local hay man. We could rent the south pastures to someone who needs grass for cattle or sheep. We could quietly take down our farm Web site. My blog could join the millions of other blogs without current postings. Letting go at this point would be the easiest thing in the world.

And the hardest.

"I can't sell them all," Melissa says. "I just can't."

And I'm thinking about fleece and yarn and making more turquoise, and about the oxytocin we get from touching animals and how much people enjoy visiting the farm, and about how important it is to raise livestock animals humanely to give people alternatives to factory-raised meat. "I can't either," I finally say.

What? What have I just said? The only explanation is my sheepishness. It's obviously terminal.

We look at our small barn and decide it can hold the three llamas, and seven sheep. We will only keep those sheep that can be bred to make more. This doesn't include the pet sheep with mastitis problems, like No. 75/101 and White Girl. The day before those two leave, I visit them, scratching behind an ear, sneaking them each a nibble of corn from my pocket. The next day Melissa faces things squarely and loads them onto the trailer. We sell Erik to two men excited about his genetics. Hearts heavy, we have now sold all the sheep but seven.

Seven sheep. Yain, tain, eddero, peddero, pitts, tayter, later.

We are now below the average flock size in Minnesota, which is ten. Seven sheep isn't a flock of sheep; it's just seven. What will we do with seven sheep? Are we going to build the flock back up, or are these seven just a temporary transition from fifty to zero? When people ask how many sheep we own, I say "our numbers are down a bit." I don't tell them what's happened. I don't tell them the number of sheep in our flock.

I can reveal my underwear size to thousands of readers in *Hit by a Farm*. I can tell a room full of total strangers that I'm gay. But to admit we only have seven sheep? That information is *much* too personal.

PART

FIVE

The Love of You Sings

Real, Not Virtual

Yes, there is Nirvana; it is in leading your
sheep to a green pasture, and in putting your
child to sleep, and in writing the last line of
your poem.

—KAHLIL GIBRAN

In today's modern society, a small farm is considered by the rest of
the country to be little more than a quaint throwback to an earlier
era. But small farms benefit society and the environment in ways
that can never be recovered in the price we charge for our lamb
or for our wool. Farming continues because, as retired professor
John Ikerd maintains, every farm has a purpose:

> The primary purpose of many small farms is to provide an op-
> portunity for open spaces, fresh air, scenic landscape, privacy,
> peacefulness, or other unique qualities of rural life. Others are

looking for a good place to raise a family . . . Others farm because they want to live close to nature; many are stewards of the land by choice, because stewardship gives purpose and meaning to their lives. For them, farming is an expression of spirituality.

Spirituality? This stops me in my tracks. But then, I've seen Melissa drop to her knees in awe over a tiny pink wildflower blooming in a grassy pasture. Time stops. Nothing is more important to her than admiring this little miracle among the grass and clover. Because she lives in the moment, Melissa's days are full of spirituality.

My own heart has beat faster to witness a lamb, looking deathly ill one evening, standing on her feet bawling for breakfast the next morning. It's a gift we are sometimes given. And on a windy day, when the breeze carries sound away from the flock, I can walk up to a sleeping lamb and gently pick him up before he knows what is happening. Usually the lamb stays quiet, a bit unnerved to find himself levitating four feet above the ground but held safely against a warm body. The best way to hold a lamb is by supporting the underside of its body with your hand and arm. This means that I am basically holding his small pounding heart in my hand. The lamb is warm and heavy and round and muscular and it seems to me a miracle that he is so healthy and so alive.

One day during a recent summer the humidity must have been 200 percent. For every molecule of oxygen in the air, there are two molecules of water. Step outside, walk ten feet, and you're drenched. Thunderclouds build gray to the west, and I want to get the mail at the end of our 600-foot driveway. So I walk slowly, admiring the approaching storm, and listening to the silence. The moisture has muffled all sound: no cars, no people, no dogs, only birds. I smell something as I walk down the driveway, but my brain's too focused on helping my current editing client choose a better title for his novel.

I retrieve the mail and start back to the house. That's when I begin to breathe more deeply. I inhale again and stop. My sense of smell isn't that great, thanks to a long season of allergies. But this? This is incredible.

After a few more deep breaths, I choke up, and for the first time in a long time, it has nothing to do with Elvis.

It's the scent. Nature has finally gotten my attention and I look down into our neighbor's alfalfa field, which runs along our driveway. The alfalfa is in bloom, the dark blue-purple flowers sending out bursts of scent. The smell doesn't blow away, but hangs there, captured by the humid air. The entire planet must smell this way.

My life is full of colorful surprises, thanks to Melissa. The morning glories she has planted along the nearby fence now bloom a rich purple. Across the driveway the cardinal creeper has climbed the legs of the fuel tank and produced delicate, bright red flowers. Melissa has a "thing" for flowers, so all summer long she distributes blossoms in small bud vases throughout the house. I often sit down at my computer to find a tiny vase with a single black-eyed susan in it, or a bright pink cosmos. There are times when living with a detail-oriented person is sweet indeed.

Then there's the day I'm wearing clean clothes (non-barn clothes) so we can attend the current film showing at our town's 1921 movie theater. We've been trying for two weeks, failing every night because of some farming issue, but tonight's the night. Then I remember I haven't fed the lamb in the barn. The ewe doesn't have enough milk for both twins, so I'm feeding one.

I stand in the barn in my clean clothes, trying not to touch anything as the lamb drinks enthusiastically from the bottle. Suddenly the heavens open up and rain pounds the roof. Oh, great.

But when the rain lets up a bit, I look out the barn door, and see the most incredible double rainbow arching across the sky. It's perfect, and I wish I could tell Melissa about it but she's in the house. By the time the lamb finishes the bottle, the rainbow has faded away and the rain has stopped. I walk back to the house, miraculously still clean and dry.

Inside Melissa is pacing. "Where were you? I wanted to show you the double rainbow." I love that after so many years, we still want to show each other the beautiful things we see.

Wave of the Future

Cultivators of the earth are the most valuable
citizens. They are the most vigorous, the most
independent, the most virtuous, and they are
tied to their country, and wedded to its liberty
and interests by the most lasting bonds.

—THOMAS JEFFERSON

Americans are ruthless when it comes to discarding the obsolete,
or the *perceived* obsolete, and sheep certainly fall into this category.
But then I stumble upon a paper called "Livestock, Ethics, and
Quality of Life" in the *Journal of Animal Science* that describes the
Five Eras of Agriculture. When I combine what I've learned about
the history of sheep with the Five Eras of Agriculture, I realize that
Melissa and I are part of the Fifth Era, the wave of the future. Cool.

According to the article, written by J. Hodges, the First Era of
Agriculture was hunting and gathering. I think this era must have

235

been rough on our hominid ancestors because they hunted animals that ran faster and had sharper teeth and actual claws. This made staying alive a bit of a struggle, but luckily early humans realized that hanging out with other humans made more sense than the "every hominid for himself" approach. Because we lacked the skills to bring down large game ourselves, we'd gather in groups, wait until the lions and leopards abandoned the carcasses and then we'd eat the bones, which were full of fatty acids very good for growing better brains. (Stealing the food killed by other predators was a useful little survival technique our ancestors practiced, known as kleptoparasitism.)

Second came the Domestication Era, when nomads settled down and domesticated a number of species, using them to provide power, food, manure, and milk. The sheep, I'm pleased to say, was one of the first mammals to be domesticated. As a result, life got better for both humans and sheep. The livestock received food and water, and protection from scary wild animals. In return, humans had milk and meat and hides for huts and clothing. They learned to collect water by leaving fleece out overnight, then wringing out the dew the next morning. They figured out that sheepskin, if stretched really thin, made a great writing surface, so it was used for stationery and books. Humans ate better, dressed better, and wore warmer clothes, which enabled them to expand into colder regions of the world.

Things continued this way for 10,000 years or so, then in the eighteenth century came the Third Era: Steam Power and Fossil Fuel. Livestock were needed less for power, and more for meat. Nearly everything having to do with sheep and wool and textiles became automated. Working with our hands became a sign of class, not of skill. Farming and sheep were *so* last century, or more accurately, *so* last *ten* centuries.

The twentieth century ushered in the Fourth Era: Intensification. What characterizes this era? As Hodges wrote, "Animals [are] increasingly seen as disposable resources in large scale specialized food production systems." This era has led to lower meat costs, increased meat production, and less consideration for the lives of the animals.

Hodges is predicting that the next transition will be to the Fifth Era: The Quality of Life Era, in which the price of meat is no longer the only factor driving agriculture. In the twenty-first century, U.S. consumers are paying attention to food safety, nutritional value, local production, sustainable farming, the environment, and animal welfare, which means ensuring a decent life for those animals we eat.

What does life look like for a sheep in the Fifth Era? It might look like life on our farm, which, whether it survives or not, is part of a complex tapestry of farms, a weaving of human and livestock lives that goes back centuries. But we're part of a disappearing life. The number of U.S. farms peaked in 1935 at 6.8 million. Today there are a little over 2.2 million, a drop of about 70 percent. The 1980s were particularly bleak, as thousands of farms were crushed between high debt and low prices. In *The Fate of Family Farming: Variations on an American Ideal*, Ronald Jager writes of an industrial food "juggernaut" able to "swallow up entire midwestern family farm communities in a single gulp."

Jager also writes that there is good news in the struggle for the soul of agriculture. As the industrial system has increased beyond comprehension, what he calls a "countervailing resistance" has developed. "There are powerful and subversive forms of aggressive resistance stirring almost everywhere within American agriculture." It seems that Jager sees us moving toward Hodges's Quality of Life Era as well.

Sustainable farming is part of that resistance, as is its subset, organic farming. Add to that food co-ops, farmers' markets, farms that sell member subscriptions, beginning farming networks, and women's farming networks.

Women farmers, young farmers, and innovative resistance to industrial farming have, at least in the short run, slowed the rate of small farm decline. According to the 2007 Census of Agriculture, the number of farms increased between 2002 and 2007 by 4 percent. Although it's true that most of the new farms are very small, and either aren't producing a product or aren't producing much volume, at least the *idea* of farming continues to burn in people's minds and souls. And here's some good news: That same census shows that the number of sheep and goat farms are increasing. The secret's out.

In his book *A Reenchanted World: The Quest for a New Kinship with Nature*, James William Gibson writes that the future of this planet depends on how humans feel when they interact with it. So many people in the United States are estranged from nature, having lost their connection to the natural world other than through brief vacations into it. But if people can find some way to connect, some way to experience the enchantment of nature, the planet may have a chance.

Farm animals are often called "domestic" to differentiate them from "nature." But cows, pigs, sheep, goats, chickens, and ducks *are* part of nature. Even though on small farms their lives are mostly under our control (on factory farms their lives are totally controlled), farm animals still provide a rich connection to the natural world.

Smalls farms like ours represent tiny pockets of enchantment, places where you can marvel at the perfect, warm eggs chickens lay. You can watch a newborn lamb stagger over to the udder and discover it for the first time. You can watch adolescent steers kick up their heels in excitement because you've come to visit them. People appreciate nature and how everything fits together when we care for it responsibly.

I would hate to give that up.

Farmer and writer Gene Logsdon touches on why people from the city, including Melissa and me, move to rural areas and begin farms:

> Many people in farming are unhappy and don't belong there. But there are likely thousands, perhaps millions of people in urban situations who are unhappy because they belong in farming and do not know it. They have the true farmer's spirit in them—that blend of creative artistry, independence, manual skill, and love of nurturing that marks a true farmer.

Melissa was born with that spirit. I wasn't. But even though I enjoy calling myself a backup farmer and highlighting my distaste for birthing and manure, after fifteen years on the farm I begin to think that, much as a plant absorbs the flavor of the soil in which it lives, I might have absorbed a bit of this spirit myself.

Listening to Sheep

Shepherding is an ancient scientific culture
and teaches people more than they intended
to learn and brings out qualities in them
they might not attain directly through moral
ambition.

—GARRISON KEILLOR

I keep reading about middles, hoping to glean some advice I can use. I don't find much. Then I wonder if I have any wisdom myself to share, since I've made it through many middles. Sadly, I don't, proving it's entirely possible to reach an age without having a clue how you got there.

Where else to turn for wisdom? Memoirs just aren't helping.

But then I head for the pasture. Sit next to a sheep on a summer day and you will experience a weird sort of envy. You'll want to be a sheep, if only for a few days, to get some relief from the stress of your own life. Robert Pirsig, author of *Zen and the Art of Motorcycle Maintenance*, believes that the only Zen you find on the tops of mountains is the Zen you bring there. This may be true, but at least in the quiet of the mountaintop—or the sheep pasture—you can actually *hear* your Zen. In the chaos and clattering of our lives, the voice we should be listening to is too quiet to be heard. It's the voice of a sheep.

When I listen, I discover four ideas to help the rest of my "middles"—farm, relationship, life—go more smoothly.

Yain: Slow down and focus on the basics

All sheep do is eat greens, drink plenty of water, and get enough rest. This might sound boring, but when you spend time with them, they don't seem bored at all. They seem well fed, well hydrated, and well rested. Sheep lie down when they're tired. They stand up when they're not.

Verlyn Klinkenborg writes of animals and sleep in one of his *New York Times* editorials on rural life: "What a lot of shut-eye all the other species get, and how sleep-deprived humans seem in comparison! . . . I can only wonder what it's like to be so well rested, to know that the deep pool of sleep within you . . . is filled to the brim."

Klinkenborg points out that animals do not berate themselves for closing their eyes now and then. "You are not a worse chicken for snoozing in the early morning, nor an inferior pig for napping the afternoon away in the shade beneath your house."

Sheep know there is no shame in getting the sleep they need.

Tain: Do one thing at a time

A sheep can't chew her cud and run. She can't chew her cud and talk. She can't chew her cud and Twitter or e-mail or drive or exercise or really do anything but lie there and chew. I've forgotten how to do only one thing at a time, so I'm going to try harder to find a few minutes in my day when I'm not eating, talking, reading, writing, mowing, phoning, cooking, cleaning, doing chores, or stacking wood . . . to sit there not doing anything but thinking. I might feel lazy and unproductive, but the sheep's self-esteem has remained intact, so mine should, too.

Eddero: Practice gazing

My sheep stare off down the valley. What are they looking at? They might be relaxing their eyes. Years ago I read that the only way the eye can totally relax and get a break from focusing so intently on the world is to look at the horizon. Long distances enable our eyes to take a break from the assaults of modern life.

Cities make horizon-gazing hard, but take a lesson from sheep. Find some way to gaze at the horizon. Imagine you're sitting in the grass in the warm sun with a sheep, both of you chewing your cud. On second thought, imagine the sheep is chewing her cud and you're sipping flavored coffee and eating from a sampler box of chocolates. When I remember to look up from my life and focus on the horizon, my eyes, and therefore my body and mind, relax.

Peddero: Overdose on oxytocin

We meet customers interested in purchasing meat from animals raised humanely and sustainably. We meet young kids desperate to touch a chicken, and older kids determined to touch the electric fence. We meet people interested in spinning and weaving, and people interested in sheep and llamas and small farms. These connections weave an amazing fabric between city and country, and generate their own version of Black Girl's oxytocin fix.

Sheep seem to appreciate what we do for them. I've decided that getting through the middle of a relationship requires appreciation, and lots of it. One day Melissa and I are driving up to the Twin Cities and I'm miserable. My changing metabolism and hormone replacement pills and other factors have added more weight to my frame than it has ever carried before. After a lengthy rant about my weight, my eyes fill with self-pity and I fall silent.

Melissa turns to me and rests her hand on my thigh, then says, "You know, I will always love you, even when you don't love yourself."

Just like that, the tears stop and contentment flows. "Tell me more," I say, and she does. My heart sproings and worfls. We're high on oxytocin.

Rhubarb Sauce and Candy Corn

Wise men say only fools rush in / But I can't help falling in love with you.

—"Can't Help Falling in Love,"
recorded by Anne Murray, Pearl Jam, and
someone else . . . let's see . . . what was his name?
Name's on the tip of my tongue. It rhymes with "pelvis."

The call finally comes from London, the woman dyeing our yarn. We arrange to meet in a Target parking lot for the exchange. When she opens her trunk, my eyes drink in so much color I have problems speaking intelligently. She opens a large plastic container and shows me the hand-painted yarn, now all wound in cute round balls. The fun part about hand-painted yarns is that when knit up into something, the yarn has a random color pat-

tern. In London's trunk there are over twenty different color combinations, three or four skeins of each.

This is it. Forget the greens of a lush pasture or the blues of a
clear horizon. *This* is what I want.

London opens a large plastic bag. Instead of painting these
skeins, she immersed them into vats of dye, or dye pots, in such a
way that the end result is variegated. I can barely contain my
excitement to see, peeking out from a pile of green skeins, a mass
of bright turquoise. Color. It's mine, all mine. Totally drunk now,
I nod numbly as London explains her process.

The final bag holds round balls of roving that she has dyed a
riot of pastel colors—green, orange, pink, and lavender. She hands
me a sample of the yarn she's spun from the roving, and I know I
must duplicate this myself.

That night I lay out all the skeins on the dining room table.
Friends from California are visiting, and our neighbors stop by to
pick up eggs, so I pour everyone glasses of wine and give them the
task: Help me name these colors.

Perhaps the wine isn't a good idea. The color names begin in-
nocuously enough—Grass Green, Sky Blue—but then we head into
areas that might make the yarn a little hard to market, especially as
we struggle to stick with farm-related colors. Fresh Chicken Poop.
Twice-Chewed Cud. Dried Placenta. Clearer heads than ours are
needed to name the yarn.

A few days later I attack the job myself. The hand-dyed yarns
glow with names like Coral, Purple Rain, Tuscan Gold, Autumn
Leaves, My Blue Jeans, Rhubarb Sauce, and of course, Bright
Turquoise. The hand-painted yarns become Lemon Lime, Lilac
Bush, Mother Earth, Watermelon, Pink Roses, and Candy Corn.

Not sure what to expect, I photograph all the yarn, dis-appointed the camera can't accurately capture the turquoise, and put the yarn up for sale on my blog.

Within a month, I've sold almost all of it, and those who come to the blog too late urge me to make more. I love our sheep. I love the farm itself. But this? It's beyond my expectations. Soft pastels. Bright colors. Warm yarn that feels good in my hands. Amazing wool. Ah, the love of you sings and binds so that the hearts of those who make merchandise of you are not able to disengage themselves from you.

Oops.

Freaks 'R' Us

I am a yarn whore!

—(I'M NOT SURE ANYONE HAS ACTUALLY SAID THIS,
BUT I'LL BET EVERY FIBER FREAK HAS AT LEAST *THOUGHT* IT.)

Yes, it's true. I've fallen down the rabbit hole of fiber freakiness. I knit a sock from the skein of our yarn I named Minnesota Fields, a mix of blues and greens and browns. I can't believe how good it feels to hold the yarn and wrap it around the needles and slide it through the loops.

Fiber people have a word for when a yarn feels really satisfying as you knit it. It's called "hand," as in "it has a nice hand." So, here we are, with only seven sheep, and I find myself saying, even though it sounds a bit suggestive, that our sheep "give good hand." Of course they do so in an entirely healthy and platonic and non-gross sort of way.

I finish that sock, and immediately knit a second. Then I perform a scientific test. Wool is supposed to repel odor rather than absorb it, so I wear my Minnesota Fields socks an alarming number of days in a row. And when I check, the socks are as fresh as a Minnesota field. It's true—wool doesn't absorb odors.

I knit a pair in the Pink Roses yarn, a mix of pink and hot pink and tan and yellow. I resolve to be one of those people who wear socks with open-toed Birkenstock sandals so that everyone can see my socks.

Okay, I've *always* been one of those geeks who wear socks with Birkenstocks, only now the socks totally rock. Besides, why hide such cool socks? I recently sat in the Colorado Springs airport guarding our bags while Melissa went in search of water. (Yes, even though I gripe about not traveling, we do get out now and then. Thanks, Bonnie, for farm sitting!) As I sat there in my Pink Roses socks and Birkies, a well-dressed, not-yet-middle-aged woman, perhaps in her mid-fifties, stopped in front of me.

"Excuse me, but did you knit those socks?"

I sat up straighter. "Why, yes, I did."

"They're just lovely. The yarn is gorgeous. Do you mind if I ask where you purchased it?"

I looked around for Melissa. She was never going to believe this conversation, which sounded like it had been scripted by a knitter overly fond of her socks. "I didn't purchase it," I said. "The yarn came from my sheep."

The woman arched an eyebrow, impressed. I should have had a business card to hand her. This is an interesting marketing idea. Perhaps I'll just fly from airport to airport in my open-toed sandals, selling yarn to traveling knitters.

My goofy pride in my socks only grows. Then one day I stand at the counter of our local yarn shop and when the sales clerk asks what I've been knitting recently, I say "socks."

"Oh, those seem so hard," she says.

"No, they're not. And I'm knitting them out of our sheep's wool." Then, shockingly, as if I've suddenly been possessed by the Spirit of Inappropriate Behavior, I slip off my Birkie and hoist my foot up onto the chest-high counter. "See?"

"Oh," the woman says, a bit alarmed.

Ten years ago when I had my midlife crisis, I'd celebrated its end by getting that mermaid tattoo that I'd showed off a bit too freely. As I stand there with my foot on the counter, déjà vu threatens to bowl me over. I carefully lower my foot before I strain something, then I apologize. But I'm excited. I feel the same way as I did with the tattoo. I've moved through some hard years of confusion and tension and crying over Elvis.

Winifred Gallagher writes in *Rapt: Attention and the Focused Life*, "You cannot always be happy, but you can almost always be focused, which is the next best thing." Our lives are fashioned by what we pay attention to. Our future will be created by what we choose to focus on. Gallagher advises that if you were to direct your focus more consciously, "your life would stop feeling like a re-action to stuff that happens to you and become something that you create—not a series of accidents, but a work of art."

I've let the farm shape my life, but in a reactive way. Even though I was involved in all the decisions, there'd been nothing to really make the farm mine. But now there is. I can focus on wool and yarn and dyeing yarn and selling yarn. Fiber is the thread, literally, that I can pick up from the farm's last fifteen years and carry with me into the future.

One afternoon Melissa and I are walking the dogs down the driveway. "We made the right decision to sell the sheep," she says.

"And we made the right decision to keep some," I add. Without sheep, how can I make more yarn?

We walk. We talk. We yell at Molly the puppy to stop rolling in the coyote droppings. We wave to Robin the border collie, who's parked himself back near the house because his heart's bad and he no longer has the oomph to walk all the way down the driveway. We let Sophie the Great Dane sniff every blade of grass.

Then we decide to keep going, and by that I don't mean keep walking, but keep farming. We're not done yet.

Sheepish and Proud

What a wonderful life I've had! I only wish I'd
realized it sooner.

—COLETTE

Spring comes, but there are no lambs this year because we didn't
breed the seven ewes before we sold Erik. We were unsure if Melissa would be recovered from the surgery in time. I miss the lambs.
I miss the Pasture Goddesses. I miss the sproinging.

We purchase another four baby calves, and I rub their fore-
heads every day as we train them to drink from the bucket instead
of from a bottle. Their front teeth look like brilliant white Chi-
clets. When their milk buckets are empty, they bang and push
them until they end up wearing the buckets as hats. This makes
me laugh every morning. I get my spring fix when I let them out
of the barn and watch them scamper through the grass, kicking up
their heels. Soon they'll be old enough to wean and move out

onto the pasture with the sheep and llamas. What a funny little diverse flock we will have then.

The seven sheep and three llamas and four steers graze quietly all summer. We buy a Corriedale ram and will introduce him to the ewes in December. Next year there will be lambs in the pasture again. In about four years we'll be back up to forty sheep. We'll resupply our meat customers. We'll build our yarn business. The farm is shifting into renewal. Sheep are good for the environment, for the clothing industry, for small farms, and for our sanity. Even Prince Charles is a friend to sheep. In January 2010, he launched the Campaign for Wool. It's part of a global campaign to raise awareness of the benefits of wool by emphasizing the natural, biodegradable, and renewable qualities of wool. And their slogan? "No Finer Feeling."

We will likely continue naming everything on the farm (except for the female sheep). We struggle with what to name the new ram, but he finally ends up Inigo Montoya ("You killed my father. Prepare to die."). Black Girl should now really be named Black-and-White Girl, because over the years the sun has lightened the fleece on her body, but why change a name she already knows?

Melissa finds a new male duck to keep Helen company and decides to name him Atal Bihari Vajpayee after the former prime minister of India. When Mr. Vajpayee was in office, we'd wake up in the morning to a public radio correspondent rattling off the guy's name so fast it made us laugh every time. Melissa calls the duck "Vajpayee," but I've altered it to something phonetically similar, Mr. Bodgepie. Either way, it's a weighty name with which to saddle any duck. For the first two months Mr. Bodgepie was here, Helen hated him and spent a great deal of energy chasing him around the barnyard. The chasing and hissing have stopped, so can the love be far behind?

We'll continue to survive the not-so-happy endings, and celebrate the happy ones. Just the other day Melissa finds our elderly llama Chachi near death on the ground, brought down by exhaustion or heat. After four days of Melissa propping him up, forcing him to drink water, and giving him shots, he's now back on his feet, unwilling to let Melissa stick him with any more needles. This is a happy ending.

As farmer John Burroughs wrote in the nineteenth century, "Cling to the farm, make much of it, put yourself into it, bestow your heart and your brain upon it, so that it shall savor of you and radiate your virtue after your day's work is done."

I don't "radiate virtue," but Melissa does. She works hard, both off and on the farm, and understands that she needs the oxytocin release that comes with caring for animals. She's firmly rooted to this life, and to this place. John Burroughs would have liked Melissa. He didn't think much of nonfarmers. "The lighter the snow, the more it drifts . . . the more frivolous the people, the more they are blown . . . into towns and cities."

Farmers tend to be weightier people. We stay put. Either by birth or personality, we become attached to a specific piece of the planet and will go to incredible lengths to be able to stay. Marilee Foster explains why farmers put up with the instability of weather and prices and animal husbandry in *Dirt Under My Nails:* "We are able to tolerate this kind of instability because we are permitted certainty about one thing, that is, if all else fails, the land, which we continually pay for with our time and labor and taxes, is ours. And when it is ours, there is not only a future for farming, but options."

I've struggled to persist as a farmer. We're told all the time that the only way to succeed at anything is to persist, but few self-help books or O *Magazine* articles explain *how* to persist. It's been fifteen years, yet Melissa and I continue to persist as farmers. Not because we're too afraid to change, or because we're wildly success- ful, but because we still learn from our mistakes, and from our animals. We've given up the idea that this farm will look perfect. Our farm is beautiful to us; we don't see that pile of old pallets waiting to be cut into firewood. We don't see the weeds, the little gash in every building left by Melissa's tractor, the banged-up equipment.

I finally figure out that persistence is a choice. It helps to admit that quitting is an option, a decision writers face every day. David Bayles and Ted Orlando make an important point about persist- ence in their book, *Art and Fear:* "Quitting is fundamentally dif- ferent from stopping. Stopping happens all the time. Quitting happens once. Quitting means not starting again—and art is all about starting again."

Therefore, even if our seven sheep look a bit silly on fifty acres, we're starting again. The farm's had some struggles. My middle's a little thicker than I'd like. I'm getting older. I slipped off the re- cycling bandwagon temporarily. Time to give myself a few baby boomer bitch slaps and get over it. No memoir or self-help book is going to help me chart the rest of my life.

Our sheep producers' association awards four bred ewes to a young person every year, and these ewes become a starter flock for kids interested in sheep. The seven sheep we have left are *our* starter flock. So every day that Melissa or I tug on our boots and walk out to the animals, we're starting again. Every day that we hold hands or make each other laugh, Muffin and Mrs. Muffin are starting again. Perhaps the secret to getting through relationships, farms, or careers is to start again every day, to find something *new* buried in the middle. Beginnings can happen anywhere, even in the middle.

I'm still sort of lost some days, which I guess is normal. Nothing is certain. I can't predict the future of this farm. It may rise dramatically like a phoenix from the ashes, or it may lumber into the air like a Muscovy duck. I'm not sure if the yarn will work as a business—plenty of others are doing the same thing. Instead, maybe we'll run a Farm Camp for Adults: "Pay $100 a Day to Work Your Bumfitt Off"! Or maybe we'll go big into beef. The point is that I don't see an RV in our immediate future. But I might see a new novel. I think I'll call it "The Love of Ewe Sings."

I finally receive my pair of wool underwear in the mail. They are heavenly. *Seriously.* If we can produce underwear this soft from wool, the possibilities are endless. I must therefore add one more item to my earlier sheepish list, an item that can be enjoyed by urban and rural alike: wool undies.

Everyone sheepish will be wearing them.

Acknowledgments

Some authors can write in a vacuum, but I would be lost without feedback from my talented writing friends. They come through for me every time. Many thanks to Cindy Rogers, Phyllis Root, Pat Schmatz, Bonnie Graves, Maggie Morris, Alice Duggan, Kathy Connelly, and JC Koepsell. I so appreciate the support and direction of my editor, Renee Sedliar, and my agent, Faye Bender. Copy editor Michele Wynn made me look amazing. (Sorry about all the lay/lie issues, and constantly misusing "while." Being so grammatically challenged makes me feel . . . well . . . sheepish, in the *traditional* sense of the word.)

Amelia Hansa, Mary Hoff, and Bonnie Mueller shared their perspectives on this story with me, and I'm grateful for all their help, courage, energy, and laughter. Annie Modesitt, Joanne Seiff, and London Nelson were incredibly helpful, and, it must be said, in large part to blame for my conversion from normal person to fiber freak. Thanks, also, to my super-speedy knitters Jan Gugino, Laura Billings Coleman, and the above-mentioned Phyllis and Kathy.

Although this farm nearly derailed my writing career all those years ago, it's redeemed itself by providing me with a wealth of writing material ever since. I am grateful, since it turns out that an easy life isn't worth writing about. Melissa sometimes asks me if I regret our decision to farm. Even though my bank account thinks fondly of our prefarming days, I myself have no regrets. I may always be a "city girl," more interested in reading and wine than in mucking out a barn or birthing lambs, but I wouldn't have missed this life—with animals, with nature, with Melissa—for anything.

Sheepish Mitten
and Hat Patterns

Designed by Annie Modesitt, author of
*Confessions of a Knitting Heretic, Romantic
Hand Knits, Knit with Courage*, and several
other knitting and crochet books

Notes: *For best fit, choose the correct hand and head circumference for your size and work to desired length.*

In each item, alternate working charted colorwork patterns #1 and #2 so placement of the motif is staggered in relation to the motif below it.

Skill Level: K 2 Easy

Mitten: To fit hand circumference 7 (8, 9, 10)" / 17.9 (20.5, 23.1, 25.6) cm, length 9.75 (10, 11.25, 12.75)" / 25 (25.6, 28.8, 32.7) cm.

Hat: To fit head circumference 17.0 (19.0, 21.0, 23.0)" / 43.6 (48.7, 53.8, 59) cm.

Fiber: Worsted weight yarn, approx 100 (110, 120, 140) yds of **each** color required for entire set.

   Yarn A: Dark Orange
   Yarn B: Purple
   Yarn C: White

Needles: One set of double pointed or 2 circular needles size: 7 US/4.5mm

Gauge: 18 sts x 24 rows = 4" / 10 cm

Notions: Darning needle, approx 12" of smooth waste yarn.

Special Stitches

K2tog-L: Knit 2 sts together so the working needle is pointing to the left as it enters the stitch (dec will slant to the left) *aka SSK, k2togTBL or s1, k1, psso*

K2tog-R: Knit 2 sts together so the working needle is pointing to the right as it enters the stitch (dec will slant to the right) *aka k2tog*

VDD—Vertical Double Decrease: Sl 2 sts as if to work k2 tog R, k1, pass slipped sts over (decrease of 2 sts)

MITTEN (Make 2)

Ribbing

With A, cast on 32 (36, 40, 44) sts and begin working in K2, P2 ribbing in the round. Place marker to note start of round. Work a total of 12 (12, 14, 16) rows, then change to color B and continue in ribbing for another 12 (12, 14, 16) rows, 24 (24, 28, 32) rows total.

Hand

Change to A and cont in 7 row charted colorwork patt #1, working contrasting motif in color C. After 7 rounds of motif, work 2 rounds in B.

Thumb Placement

Next Round: With waste yarn knit 5 (5, 6, 6) sts, then slip these waste yarn sts back onto the left needle and knit 2 more rounds in B (working across the waste yarn stitches—4 rounds of B total).

Work 7 rounds in colorwork patt #2 as below thumb placement, then work 4 more rounds in B. Break B.

Mitten Top

Alternating A and C, knit 4 rounds of A then 4 rounds of C, continue knitting even with no shaping until piece measures 3.75 (4.25, 4.75, 5.5)" / 9.6 (10.9, 12.2, 14.1) cm from thumb placement (or just beyond top of pinkie finger). Break C.

Fingertip Shaping

Next Round: Change to color B, [k2, k2togL, k10 (12, 14, 16) sts, k2togR, k2] twice—28 (32, 36, 40) sts rem.

Next Round: Cont in B, [k2, k2togL, k8 (10, 12, 14) sts, k2togR, k2] twice— 24 (28, 32, 36) sts rem.

Next Round: Change to color A [k2, k2togL, k6 (8, 10, 12) sts, k2togR, k2] twice—20 (24, 28, 32) sts rem.

Cont as est, working 2 rounds in A, 2 rounds in B and decreasing 4 sts in each round, continuing to alternate A and B every 2 rounds until 12 (12, 16, 16) sts rem.

At this point you may either bind off all sts and sew the tip together, or divide the sts into 2 groups of 6 (6, 8, 8) sts and join using the Kitchener stitch, 3 needle bind off, or any other grafting method.

Thumb

Return to the waste yarn stitches and carefully slip the 5 (5, 6, 6) sts color B sts above the waste yarn and 6 (6, 7, 7) sts below the waste yarn onto dpns or 2 circs—11 (11, 13, 13) sts.

Leaving a 8" / 10cm tail, join color B and begin working around, picking up 1 extra stitch at either edge of the thumb opening to tighten up the possible "hole" there—13 (13, 15, 15) sts total.

Cont in B only, knit in the round with no shaping until thumb measures 1.75 (1.75, 2, 2.25) sts or reaches to the bottom of the thumb nail.

Next Round: [K2togR, k1] rep to end of round, knitting 1 extra st if necessary—9 (9, 10, 10) sts rem.

Next Round: [K2tog] rep to end of round, knitting 1 extra st if necessary—5 (5, 5, 5) sts rem.

Next Round: [K2tog] rep to end of round, knitting 1 extra st if necessary—3 (3, 3, 3) rem.

Draw yarn through rem sts and tie off end.

Finishing

Weave in ends, using tails to sew up any holes around the thumb base.

HAT

Garter Cuff

With color B cast on 80 (88, 96, 104) sts, join and knit 1 round in color B, place marker to note start of round.

[With A knit 1 round, then purl 1 round, change to B and knit 1 round, then purl 1 round] rep 5 (6, 6, 7) times to create a total of 10 (12, 12, 14) rows, or 5 (6, 6, 7) purl "ridge stripes."

Sideband

With C, begin knitting 7 row charted colorwork patt #1, working contrasting motif in color B. Repeat motif 20 (22, 24, 26) times around all hat stitches. Knit 4 rounds in B.

Continuing in B and C as est, repeat last 11 rounds 1 (1, 2, 2) times more, a total of 22 (22, 33, 33) rows rounds in pattern / stripe design, or until side of hat reaches about 2" / 5cm above ear tip.

Tip Shaping

Join A and begin knitting 7 row charted colorwork patt, working contrasting motif in color C. Repeat motif 20 (22, 24, 26) times around all hat stitches. Break C.

Join B and knit 1 round in B.

Next Round: With B [k17 (19, 21, 23), VDD] 4 times—72 (80, 88, 96) rem. Knit 1 round in B.

Next Round: With B [k15 (17, 19, 21), VDD] 4 times—64 (72, 80, 88) rem. Break B.

Join A and knit 1 round in A.

Next Round: With A [k13 (15, 17, 19), VDD] 4 times—56 (64, 72, 80) rem.

Cont decreasing 8 sts as established in every round, working only with A until only 8 sts rem. Draw yarn through last 8 sts and tie off, weaving in end.

Finishing

Weave in loose ends and steam block hat.

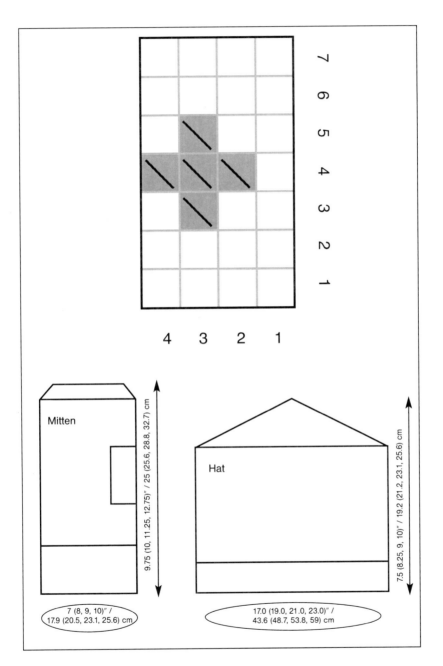